T0334571

Cambridge Elements ≡

Elements in the Problems of God
edited by
Michael L. Peterson
Asbury Theological Seminary

GOD AND ASTROBIOLOGY

Richard Playford
Leeds Trinity University

Stephen Bullivant
St Mary's University and University of Notre Dame Australia

Janet Siefert
Rice University

CAMBRIDGE
UNIVERSITY PRESS

Shaftesbury Road, Cambridge CB2 8EA, United Kingdom

One Liberty Plaza, 20th Floor, New York, NY 10006, USA

477 Williamstown Road, Port Melbourne, VIC 3207, Australia

314–321, 3rd Floor, Plot 3, Splendor Forum, Jasola District Centre, New Delhi – 110025, India

103 Penang Road, #05–06/07, Visioncrest Commercial, Singapore 238467

Cambridge University Press is part of Cambridge University Press & Assessment, a department of the University of Cambridge.

We share the University's mission to contribute to society through the pursuit of education, learning and research at the highest international levels of excellence.

www.cambridge.org
Information on this title: www.cambridge.org/9781009478656

DOI: 10.1017/9781009296175

When citing this work, please include a reference to the DOI 10.1017/9781009296175

First published 2024

A catalogue record for this publication is available from the British Library.

ISBN 978-1-009-47865-6 Hardback
ISBN 978-1-009-29614-4 Paperback
ISSN 2754-8724 (online)
ISSN 2754-8716 (print)

God and Astrobiology

Elements in the Problems of God

DOI: 10.1017/9781009296175
First published online: January 2024

Richard Playford
Leeds Trinity University

Stephen Bullivant
St Mary's University and University of Notre Dame Australia

Janet Siefert
Rice University

Author for correspondence: Stephen Bullivant, Stephen.bullivant@stmarys.ac.uk

Abstract: The perception that life on other planets would be problematic for religious people, and indeed for religion itself, is a long-standing one. It is partially rooted in fact: astrobiological speculations have, on occasion, engendered religious controversies. Historical discussions are often far more nuanced, and less one-sided than often imagined. 'Exotheology' is a lively subdiscipline within several religious traditions.

This Element offers a wide-ranging introduction to the multifarious 'problems of God and astrobiology', real and perceived. It covers major topics within Christian theology (e.g., creation, incarnation, salvation), as well as issues specific to Judaism, Islam, Buddhism, and Hinduism. It also discusses the very different perspectives offered by other (non) religious traditions, including Mormonism, various 'alien-positive' new religious movements (e.g., Heaven's Gate, Scientology, Raëlism), and the 'Ancient Astronaut' theories popularized by Erich von Däniken and the History channel's *Ancient Aliens*.

Keywords: astrobiology, aliens, extraterrestrial, God, religion

ISBNs: 9781009478656 (HB), 9781009296144 (PB), 9781009296175 (OC)
ISSNs: 2754-8724 (online), 2754-8716 (print)

Contents

1 'Irreconcileable Inconsistencies'? Introducing the Problems

> It only remains for me now to address one class of persons; they are perhaps the most difficult to satisfy, not because my reasoning is inconclusive, but because they feel themselves privileged to disregard the best arguments: I am speaking of scrupulous people who may imagine religion is endangered by placing inhabitants anywhere but on earth ...
>
> —Fontenelle, 'Preface', *Conversations on the Plurality of Worlds* (1686)

The above quotation is instructive here for two reasons. Firstly, note the date; written a good three-and-a-half centuries ago. Bernard de Fontenelle was a leading French essayist, and what we might call today 'pop science writer', at a time of significant scientific innovation. During his forty-two-year stint as Secretary to the *Academie des sciences*, its membership included Giovanni Cassini (after whom NASA's Saturn probe would later be named), Gottfried Leibniz, Isaac Newton, Jacques Bernoulli, and Edmund Halley. Fontenelle's popular *Conversations on the Plurality of Worlds* is written as a series of dialogues between a philosopher and a young noblewoman. Among much else, it popularized new astronomical thinking about the stars being Suns, uncountably large in number, vast distances away, and replete with their own planetary systems. It also argued for the likelihood of the moons and planets of our own and other solar systems being home to intelligent life: 'we conclude from the earth being inhabited that other bodies of the same nature must be so too' ([1686] 1803: 87).

Fontenelle's further speculations often veer (even more?) into the fantastical, and indeed the 'problematical' (his arguing from analogy yields racist comments about the inhabitants of the planets nearer the Sun – and thus more akin to the hotter regions of Earth – in line with common European ideas of the time (e.g., [1686] 1803: 84–5). Yet evidently, there is nothing terribly novel about serious astrobiological speculation, blending both state-of-the-art scientific information with a good deal of philosophical and literary imagination. In fact, there was nothing especially novel about this in the seventeenth century either: such subjects have been debated on and off, with a wide variety of conclusions drawn, for at least two and half thousand years (Dick 1982; Crowe 1997; Roush 2020: 15–38; Connes 2020). Fontenelle is just one example, from one particular time and place, of such debates flaring up for a period. Truly, there is nothing new under the Suns.

Secondly, note that Fontenelle is keen to pre-empt specifically religious objections to such ideas. Or rather, he is keen to pre-empt religious *objectors*: such people who reject 'the best arguments' (i.e., Fontenelle's own), out of fears that they might undermine, or otherwise impinge upon, theological convictions. Fontenelle himself thinks that all such difficulties can be sidestepped by clarifying that whomsoever inhabit other worlds, they are not *humans*, and thus not of 'the posterity of Adam': 'no more need be said; every imaginable difficulty is included in this' ([1686] 1803: xv). Why this is so, Fontenelle demurs to explain. Nevertheless, it is not his religious *readers* he worries about: 'the following conversations will be objected to only by those who have never read them. But will this consideration suffice to deliver me from the fear of censure? No; it rather gives me cause to apprehend objections from every side' ([1686] 1803: xvi).

Fontenelle's expectation of religious disquiet is, likewise, by no means unique. Like him, some writers on this topic anticipate it, but think it is ultimately misguided (often going to much greater efforts to explain why). Others actively court it. Writing a century after Fontenelle, the Anglo-Franco-American – he lived in, and made his mark on, all three countries – philosopher Thomas Paine addressed the topic at length in his best-selling pamphlet *The Age of Reason*. Paine's overall argument is fairly subtle. A convinced Deist, he advances theological arguments for believing that the innumerable worlds known to astronomers surely must be inhabited: 'As therefore the Creator made nothing in vain . . .' (1794: 45). On the basis of this, he then argues that the fact that:

> God created a plurality of worlds, at least as numerous as what we call stars, renders the Christian system of faith at once little and ridiculous; and scatters it in the mind like feathers in the air. The two beliefs cannot be held together in the same mind; and he who thinks that he believes both, has thought but little of either. (1794: 40)

The precise arguments Paine offers for positing 'irreconcileable inconsistencies between the real word of God existing in the universe, and that which is called the *word of God* [i.e., the Bible]' (1794: 47) need not detain us here. Versions of several of them, repeated and refined by later authors, will be dealt with in the sections to come. Suffice it to say that many philosophers and theologians – before, then, and since – have disagreed with Paine on one or both of his main argumentative moves. Some reject his view that the heavens must surely be inhabited, and therefore see no inconsistencies to reconcile. Others accept the possibility, and perhaps the probability, of Paine's 'cheerful idea of a society of worlds' (1794: 46), but think that, while this would indeed throw up some interesting issues, none is insuperable when properly thought through.

Whose God(s)?

Already we see the suggestion that different religious or theological systems might handle the (hypothesized) existence of life elsewhere in the universe rather differently. Fontenelle supposes that thoughtful, enlightened religious believers should have no trouble, but ignorant, dogmatic ones will: though he doesn't specify to which specific religions or denominations either group tends to belong. Meanwhile Paine thinks that his own (Deist) theology is fully supportive of the prospect, but that others' (Christian) theology soon runs into deep, indeed fatal, difficulties.

Thinking about the general theme of God, or gods, and astrobiology is not the exclusive preserve of Christian or (post-Christian) Deist cultures. How could it be? Religion and astronomy seem to have interacted in all manner of close, complex ways throughout human history. The 'heavens' have perhaps always been understood as having religious significance. This is certainly true of special celestial events: the comet taken to signify Julius Caesar's advent among the Roman gods in 44 BC (Pandey 2013); the Zoroastrian *magi*'s interest in the 'Star of Bethlehem' (Matthew 2.1–11), whose explication has exercised thinkers as diverse as Origen (*Contra Celsum*, I.lviii–lx), Johannes Kepler (Burke-Gaffney 1937), and Arthur C. Clarke (1955); the Hale-Bopp comet that triggered mass-suicides among followers of the Heaven's Gate 'UFO religion' in 1997 (see Section 5). Note too the fact that (probable) meteoritic rocks have been accorded great religious significance in various traditions. In ancient Rome, the primary cultic objects of both the 'Great Mother' goddess Cybele and the Syrian sun-god Elagabalus were imposing black stones, the latter explicitly believed to have 'come down from Zeus' (Herodian, *Histories*, 5.3). Islamic tradition records that the famous Black Stone of the Kaaba in Mecca, which was also venerated in pre-Islamic times, 'came down from paradise' (*Jami` at-Tirmidhi*, 877).[1]

But it is arguably all the truer of the painstaking observing and calculating necessary for establishing astronomy as a genuine science. Major prehistoric ritual sites – England's Stonehenge (c. 3000–2000 BC); North America's 'medicine wheels' like the one at Majorville in Alberta (c. 3200 BC); Japan's Ōyu Stone Circles (c. 2000–1500 BC) – were built to align with solstices and equinoxes (Burl 1983; Renfrew 2007: chap. 9). The fixing of the Egyptian and Babylonian calendars was at once a religious and a scientific enterprise (Chapman 2002: 57–74). In classical Islam, the founding and funding of observatories were motivated both by dreams of 'pure science', and the practicalities of knowing *precisely* when, and in what direction, to pray (Mahsood 2009: chap. 9; Al-Khalili 2010: 206). Sure, these confluences of religion and astronomy (often enough in the same people) need not prompt thoughts regarding the possible existence of life 'out there', and if so, of its implications for existing religious ideas. But equally, it would be very surprising if it had not sometimes done.

There is only so much ground one can cover within a single Element. Some of the 'problems' discussed in what follows will be broadly relevant to the three 'Abrahamic' traditions of Judaism, Christianity, and Islam (and, *mutatis mutandis*,

---

[1] See https://sunnah.com/tirmidhi:877.

to any other traditions affirming a single creator God). Others will be specific to particular doctrinal commitments in Christian or Islamic thought, for example. Where relevant, though, we will point readers to distinctively similar or different 'takes' in other major religious traditions, for example in Buddhism or Hinduism, or else in a variety of smaller movements or traditions – some overtly religious (e.g., Mormonism, Scientology, Heaven's Gate, the Aetherius Society), others not (e.g., proponents of the 'Ancient Astronaut Hypothesis').

In keeping with other Elements in this 'Problems of God' series, our explicit focus in the following pages will be on various *problems* that arise at the intersection of religion and astrobiology. In what follows, it may be helpful to think of there being two main types that we'll be discussing. The first are problems in the sense of posing, or seeming to pose, a substantial difficulty or challenge. These are problems in the 'Houston, we have a problem' meaning of the term. For example, within the philosophy of religion, 'the problem of evil' is seen as offering a powerful counter-argument to the existence of an all-loving, all-powerful God. Problems in this hard sense of the term need not, of course, be unsolvable. Many philosophers do not think that the problem of evil, in any of its many variants, is actually insuperable (though some do). But they recognize that it is a difficult problem that any intellectually robust theology needs to have a sufficiently strong answer to (Peterson 2022; Ekstrom 2023).

But problem can also have a softer, perhaps more playful meaning, closer to a 'puzzle' or 'exercise'. Typically these are open-ended, as with a philosophical thought-experiment, where the point is to imagine various hypothetical possibilities and their implications (see Baggini 2005). Problems like this can be a helpful way to clarify one's thinking. Medieval Christian thinkers, for example, did a great deal of very technical, jargon-filled theologizing around the precise nature of the Eucharist. But they would also occasionally ask *seemingly* very simple questions too. '*Quid mus sumit?*', or 'what does the mouse eat [if it happened to nibble a consecrated Host]?', was a particularly popular one, generating many detailed answers as to whether it would eat only bread, or the Body of Christ, or both, or something else (Macy 1991). They were not *really* interested in the diet, material or spiritual, of rodents. But thinking through this fun problem helped to clarify, and/or explain, their metaphysical theories concerning the eucharistic species.

'Astrobiology' can and does throw up myriad problems of both kinds vis-à-vis 'God' – many, though far from all of which, we will consider in this brief survey volume. Should life ever be discovered elsewhere in the universe, then this will certainly present interesting problems in the first, hard sense for religious believers to grapple with. But even if ours is indeed a lonely universe and no other life exists, or if we could never discover it even if it did (perhaps it lived both 'a long time ago' and 'in a galaxy far, far away'?), then at least some of these problems might still be valuable in our second, thought-experiment sense. One need not believe that there actually are sentient lifeforms in another galaxy to wonder how, if Christianity is true, Jesus' death and resurrection might be relevant to them (see Section 3). Or if Islam is true, to ponder how the Qur'an might be revealed to them – and if so, in what language, and in which direction Mecca would be from where they are (Determann 2021: 13). But thinking through these kind of issues might well, as with naughty mice and eucharistic wafers, help clarify and elucidate the underlying doctrinal commitments.

This kind of 'What if ... ?' speculation is not the exclusive preserve of philosophers and theologians. Novelists and screenwriters are the real experts here. Fortunately for us, the problems of God and astrobiology have long proven irresistible to both (Brake 2013; Nahin 2014). Many of the great science fiction writers, such as Arthur C. Clarke, Frank Herbert, and Liu Cixin, and film or television franchises, including *Star Trek*, *Star Wars*, *Stargate*, and *Red Dwarf*, have engaged these topics, often in great detail. Scholars too have sometimes turned to fiction to explore such ideas, with the Anglican theologian C. S. Lewis' 'Space Trilogy' (1938, 1943, 1945), the atheist astronomer Carl Sagan's novel and movie *Contact* (1985), and the Mormon evolutionary biologist's Steven L. Peck's short stories (2015) all notable, and notably diverse, examples. We will be drawing on several of these in the pages that follow.

Structure

Having now introduced the broad topic of 'God and Astrobiology', this Element includes five further sections.

In Section 2, we state what precisely is meant by 'astrobiology', especially as the term is used in contemporary, cutting-edge scientific research (of the kind that one of us, Siefert, has been actively engaged in for many years). As we will see, what professional biologists, chemists, and astronomers are typically looking for when they speak of 'astrobiology' for is a long way from the proverbial 'little green men' and 'flying saucers' of popular ufology. While both are relevant for the purposes of this Element, it is important to be clear on the quite how wide the full spectrum here is.

Section 3 examines the implications of Extraterrestrial Intelligences (ETIs) for classical Christianity with particular attention being paid to the incarnation and soteriology, which have proven fertile ground for astrotheological speculation. Would ETIs suffer from original sin? If so, would the fact that 'God became man' be of any soteriological use or significance for them, or would God need to have become (say) Klingon, Vulcan, Romulan, Bajoran, and Ferengi too?

Building on this foundation, Section 4 expands our investigation to consider what, if any, implications the existence of extraterrestrial life – be it microbial, intelligent, or somewhere in the middle – might have for a number of the other major world religions: Judaism, Islam, Hinduism and Buddhism.

Turning many of the traditional topics on their head, Section 5 considers the possible theological problems that would arise if it were the case that *only* Earth were home to life, despite inconceivably vast time and space. Might a mostly empty, barren universe itself undermine belief in a creative God? Conversely, what of those religious traditions affirming a 'crowded universe', or making 'contact' on or by a certain date? For these traditions, it is precisely the *lack* of confirming astrobiology that poses a serious apologetic and doctrinal problem – sometimes, as we shall see, with tragic consequences.

Our sixth and final section shows the ways in which beliefs about astrobiology have been used within several broadly atheistic traditions in order to explain (away) beliefs in God. These include 'ancient astronaut' accounts of religious scriptures and phenomena (e.g., reported miracles), as popularized by writers such as Erich von Däniken and in the long-running documentary series *Ancient Aliens*, as well as naturalistic explanations of certain religious phenomena (e.g., religious experience) on analogy with sightings of UFOs, alien abduction reports, and the like.

2 What Do We Mean by Astrobiology?

A galaxy is composed of gas and dust and stars – billions upon billions of stars. Every star may be a sun to someone.

—*Carl Sagan*

What is astrobiology, you might ask? It's an odd word. It conjures up the confidence we have in astrophysics while marrying concepts of alien biology to astronomy. The problem is, as substantive as the word seems to be, it is expectant that there is more life out there than the only one we have knowledge of! Unless you are an *Ancient Aliens* believer (see Section 6), it's hard to know how to place the word and the scientific discipline in the context of real science and humankind's philosophical musings about extraterrestrial life. This section seeks to bridge the gap between those who have looked up at the stars and wondered '*am I alone?*', with those who build rockets and spectrometers to see if we are. And it's all wrapped up in this word, astrobiology.

For the astrobiologist, astrobiology is defined as the study of the origin, evolution, distribution, and future of life in the universe (Kaufman, n.d.). This is a very specific definition that is used to guide astrobiological research. We will discuss when the word was coined and how it is used to describe a twenty-first century scientific discipline. But we should note that today astrobiologists rarely include philosophical concerns in their proposals or projects. That's not to say there aren't any. It would be disingenuous not to admit that at the heart of astrobiology is the *belief* that life *in some form*, likely exists (or has existed) somewhere else in our vast universe. (Interestingly, astrobiologists are mostly agnostic in their efforts to address the opposite of that belief: if there isn't life elsewhere, why not? Of course, it's devilishly difficult to prove a negative. We consider this topic in Section 5.)

Early Beginnings

The word was likely coined in an article published in a French popular science magazine in 1935 by a Russian Jew, Ary J. Sternfeld (Briot 2012). Sternfeld was a pioneer of astronautics who wrote numerous scientific books and papers. He was, among many things, insightful. Sternfeld's philosophical explanations and, curiously, his conception of astrobiology (from French *astrobiologie*) are very similar to the way astrobiology exists as a discipline today.

The early beginnings of astrobiology came out of the space race, the Cold War, and burgeoning research that hinted at discoverable knowledge of how life on Earth got started. In 1953, Stanley Miller and Harold Urey published the results of their now famous experiment. Miller and Urey simulated the chemical conditions of early Earth by filling a flask with a solution of methane, ammonia, hydrogen, and water. An electrical charge was sent through the milieu (simulating lightning) and an analysis of the resulting black goo showed that some amino acids had been formed. Amino acids are one of the building blocks of life and it is very difficult to find a self-organizing way for those to be formed on early Earth.

The then new US space program embraced their results and instituted the Exobiology Program. With exobiology funding beginning in 1959 and the creation of instruments designed to detect microbial life in extraterrestrial environments, NASA began the initial investment in what would become one of the defining concepts of astrobiology. *Exobiology* laid the groundwork for what would be a broader approach to studying life in the universe, that is, the discipline now known as *astrobiology*. By 1995, with exobiology moving forwards, and with researchers in planetary sciences and astrophysics making progress, there was a need for a more interdisciplinary acumen to be brought to the table. Thus, NASA's Astrobiology program was formed! Over the next two decades, US Astrobiology programs would jumpstart international partnerships, witness universities unveiling degree programs in the discipline, and US centric multi-discipline, multi-institutional centres of astrobiology were created and aided by internet communication technology.

Philosophers were hardly idle, although not usually directly involved in astrobiology research. In an industry where research initiatives are used to inform multibillion-dollar space missions, philosophical and theological concerns are reasonably minimal. If you should attend an astrobiology conference or a research conference centred around the origins of life, the closest you would get to hearing any philosophy *might* be the debate on exactly what we might be looking for. Defining *life* turns out to be problematic. Viruses, Earth's poster child for this conundrum, are just the tip of the iceberg. If we aren't sure whether to put viruses in the alive category or not, imagine how difficult the argument is if we are trying to define what life might be made of or look like in another solar system or galaxy. Would life have to have the same elements that Earth-based life uses? Would it need to reproduce and use some kind of evolutionary process to produce diversity and adaptive potential? Most of the philosophical arguments were ones that helped to hone in on just how difficult it was going to be to find life, not discounting the problem that we might not recognize it even if we saw it.

A good example of the sorts of philosophical arguments and considerations being formulated throughout this time is the anthropic principle, also known as the 'observation selection effect', first proposed in 1957 by Robert Dicke. This principle stipulated that the range of possible observations that we could make about the universe is limited by the fact that observations could only happen in a universe capable of developing intelligent life in the first place. Supporters of this idea argue that there are fundamental properties of our universe that seem finely tuned for life. SETI (Search for Extraterrestrial Intelligence) spent a good portion of the late twentieth century scanning extremely small portions of the night sky for signals from intelligent civilizations that Earth-based satellite dishes could detect. It was very much like trying to find a needle in a haystack, but you aren't sure where the haystack is, or if it even houses a needle!

Perhaps unsurprisingly, their findings, or lack thereof, were largely disappointing. As a result, the focus and funding of astrobiology's search for life quickly opted out of searching for intelligent aliens and started searching for ones much smaller, microscopic in fact. It was becoming clear that life on planet Earth would sustain itself nicely enough if all we had were microbial communities. In fact, geology was showing that it is likely the case that this is all there was here for at least a good portion of a billion years or so. Add to that the fact that microbial life here exhibited a range of bizarre environmental extremes and you've got a reasonable shot at finding really mini ETs.

Drake, Fermi, and the Prime Directive

THE DRAKE EQUATION

$$N = R* \times f_p \times n_e \times f_l \times f_i \times f_c \times L$$

N = the number of extraterrestrial civilizations with which human beings could communicate

$R*$ = average rate at which stars form in our galaxy

f_p = fraction of stars with planets

n_e = number of planets that could potentially support life per star that has planets.

f_l = fraction of planets that could potentially support life that actually go on to develop life

f_i = fraction of life-supporting planets that develop intelligent life

f_c = fraction of intelligent species that develop the capacity for interstellar communication

L = average length of time that such communicative civilizations are active

In 1961, Frank Drake came up with the Drake Equation, which provided further argument that the prospect of finding life was not as hopeful we might have thought, even the microbial kind. Combining mathematical terms in an equation meant to describe the environmental conditions spanning our place in the solar system, in our galaxy and in the universe, the Drake Equation did provide a better illustration of what life needed galactically. However, it reiterated just how special our locality was for generating life (at least life as we know it). Peter Ward and Donald E. Brownlee then added a number of additional terms to the original Drake Equation to formulate their 'Rare Earth' hypothesis (see Ward and Brownlee 2000), providing an even more pessimistic look into the chances of intelligent life. Ward would have been the darling of evangelicals except that he claimed no allegiance to any faith-based argument in his conclusions.

Then there was Fermi. The Fermi paradox states that even though our universe is unfathomably gigantic we haven't had any sign of intelligent life (dead or alive) from any part of it. Why? Recently, Cai et al. performed a 'statistical estimation of the occurrence of extraterrestrial intelligence in the in Milky Way Galaxy' (2021), and it was a bleak tweak to the Fermi paradox. The take away from this study was that any civilization technically sophisticated enough to make contact likely would self-annihilate before doing so.

There is another area of quasi-philosophical concern that the astrobiology community embraced. *Star Trek's* moral sensitivity for life elsewhere as articulated in the Prime Directive was the guiding principle prohibiting Starfleet's members from interfering with the natural development of alien civilizations. Just so, astrobiology invested in a somewhat similar philosophy, if not nearly as optimistic in who or what we might encounter. The possibility of forwards and backwards contamination with space exploration as the vector has been a global concern since the early 50s. NASA responded in a practical and politically astute way. US tax dollars support a Planet Protection Officer and have done so for several decades (OSMA). This is likely the most direct way in which philosophical concerns play out in practical ways within the astrobiology research community.

Conclusion

But this section is about astrobiology writ large. We have provided a snapshot of how scientists think philosophically about extraterrestrial life and how the research has been driven by these philosophies. With that in mind we need to address what difference does it make to humanity should we find evidence of life? How do the goals of astrobiology intersect with humankind's wonder, are we alone? Does it matter that all we are looking for is simple life? Given the near-term global reach for human colonization and exploration of our near stellar neighbours (the moon and Mars) as well as an ever-increasing understanding of what we mean by extrasolar habitable worlds, this conversation is relevant and timely.

Humans have always been curious about what lay in the stars just as we have always wondered about who we are in relation to how or why those stars came to be. Every culture has a creation story to tell. Will the results of missions and research driven by astrobiology inform or detract from any of those stories, and in the case of Christianity, what will be required to explain a creation that is not of Earth. Will we need to reinterpret scripture? Will Jesus atone for aliens? Are aliens made in the image of God?

Despite the argument provided here that astrobiology is concentrating on microbial evidence, either as fossils or as agents of change in purely physical and chemical driven environments (spectra), the public often imagines ETI as science fiction has depicted them. Science fiction has not only driven how ETIs could look but in many cases how the fictional aliens' theology or philosophy might impact our own views, and vice versa. No matter the level of sophistication of special effects, odd number of appendages or eyes, reptilian looking aliens, it's always been surprising to me that in an effort to show a different kind of biology, most of these artistic imaginings are based upon bilateral body plans. This kind of body plan is certainly a very complex, well evolved way of organizing cells on Earth. It shows the prejudice we have that ETIs aren't that much different than us, even if they do have scales. The only science fiction that the actual astrobiologist among us (i.e., Siefert) can remember that vaguely resembles what astrobiologists look for now would be *The Blob*, a 1950s movie she saw at a drive-in theatre and still finds a little bit scary.

So, what will be the worry for the believer or the atheist if we find a biosignature in the Goldilocks zone of a far distant planet? What if we find microbial fossils on Mars? The easiest way out for theologians would be if we found life on Mars with DNA or RNA. We'd be tasked with figuring out how life is contaminating or being contaminated inadvertently. It would be rather bad news for our Planet Protection Office. It's much more interesting (in terms of difficulty) for scientists and preachers if there is some information system that is completely different than ours. As it stands now, astrobiology isn't likely to find ETI with an answer to cosmic questions or whether our creator revealed himself. Microbes don't do words. As far as we know...

3 Christianity: Incarnation, Redemption, and Soteriology

The possibility of intelligent extraterrestrial life is at once exciting and terrifying. In part, it is exciting because of the opportunities it might present should we encounter it. It might provide currently undreamt of opportunities for learning, growth, trade, technological development, artistic and cultural exchange, and so on. At the same time, it is also terrifying. A cursory overview of history shows that when 'alien' human cultures come into contact there is the very real risk of violence, prejudice, exploitation, and persecution. How much more so when we are dealing with a completely alien extraterrestrial species? Another reason for our trepidation is that throughout most of our history human beings have been the dominant species on our planet, and our current technological sophistication allows us to both dominate and, sadly all too often, destroy ecosystems. If we were to encounter extraterrestrials our technological dominance could be overturned in an instant, and our time as the dominant species in our various environments could come to an end.

Alien 'Humans'

For these reasons, it is hardly surprising that the possibility of extraterrestrial life holds a fascination for us in the twenty-first century. There is, however, another reason for our preoccupation with alien life. Often, when examining these topics, individuals will ask: Are we alone in the universe? This question illuminates many hidden assumptions about ourselves as a species. For example, strictly speaking, the answer to the question 'are we alone in the universe?' is a resounding 'No!' We share our planet with millions of other species, both weird and wonderful, so we are very much *not* alone. And yet this question seems to imply that we *feel* alone. Perhaps this shows us that whilst we might appreciate the company of the various animal and plant species with whom we share this planet, perhaps we sense an important distinction between us and them. This distinction between us and them we can label our humanity.

There is insufficient space here to fully examine what it means to be human, but we may assume that it is something more than merely being a member of the species *Homo sapiens*. Here, let us assume that when we talk about our 'humanity', we are talking about our intelligence, creativity, capacity for love, art, music, and so on. As Oderberg explains, the sorts of things that make us human include:

> the capacity for such things as: abstract thought . . . language; . . . knowledge of finality; the conscious ordering of ends or objectives; development of and adherence to a life plan; reflection, meditation . . . a moral life . . . humour, irony, aesthetic sensibility, the creation and maintenance of families and political societies . . . we all know the sorts of things we rational animals are capable of. (2014: 216)

Oderberg's use of the term 'rational animal(s)' is, of course, referring to Aristotle's definition of humanity. This definition illuminates why many of us are fascinated by the possibility of extraterrestrials and why we can feel dissatisfied sharing creation only with earthly non-human animals. This is because, whilst we share an animal nature with our fellow terrestrial creatures (having a body, needing to take in sustenance, being vulnerable to damage and disease, needing to reproduce, and so on), we are importantly different to them because we alone are rational. With that rationality comes a host of abilities which are unique to us as human beings (as listed earlier) and in this sense we *are* alone. Only we create art, music, literature, and engage in science, mathematics, abstract thought, and so on.

If we accept the Aristotelian definition of man as a rational animal, then it follows that, in at least this sense of the word, intelligent extraterrestrials would also be 'human'. Why? Because like us they will have bodies (even if they are very unusual bodies by terrestrial standards) and, more importantly, they will be rational. As a result, they will share some and perhaps all of those really important characteristics that make us what and who we are as a species and as individuals. Therefore, if we discover another intelligent species out there, there will be a sense in which we are no longer *alone*, and perhaps this explains our fascination with this possibility.

Some may find the idea that ETIs are also 'human' absurd. Humans, they may say, have two arms and two legs, are warm-blooded mammals, are a carbon-based lifeform, and so on. Barring some enormous cosmic coincidence, or divine providence, an extraterrestrial species is not going to share in these features and therefore they are not human. Arguably, however, this disagreement is merely terminological. Certainly, *Homo sapiens* (normally) have two arms and two legs, are warm-blooded mammals, and so on, but when we talk about 'humanity' in a broader sense there is nothing to necessitate all human beings sharing in these features. However, if the use of the words 'humans', 'humanity', and so on, simply sounds too strange to the reader when considering ETIs, then one might simply replace those terms with ones such as rational animality, intelligent animals, embodied persons, and so on. The main point here is that intelligent extraterrestrials will be importantly like us in certain respects.

At the same time, as already alluded to, intelligent extraterrestrials would also likely be very different to us given that they would have evolved in a very different environment. As a result, they will likely appear strange and exotic. This only adds to their fascination and mystery.

We can now see the philosophical dimension of the problem posed by intelligent extraterrestrials. They are both very much like us, whilst also being (very literally) 'alien'. This means that the possibility of their existence throws up a host of existential and philosophical questions for every single one of us as terrestrial human beings, regardless of our differing religious beliefs or, indeed, lack thereof.

Creation, Revelation, Redemption

For the Christian, however, there are a host of additional problems raised by the possibility of intelligent extraterrestrials. Losch and Krebs (2015) have divided these into three categories. These are creation, revelation, and redemption (which includes issues of both incarnation and salvation). Partly due to limits on space, and partly because they are easily dealt with, the first two will be discussed here only very briefly.

With regard to creation, some may ask whether, if they exist, God created intelligent extraterrestrials. This is easily answered in the affirmative. Genesis 1:1 states that 'In the beginning God created the heavens and the earth' (NIV) and because of this and other similar passages in the Bible mainstream

Christianity teaches that God is the creator everything that exists (see, e.g., Catholic Church 1997: paras 279–301). Therefore, if there are extraterrestrials (intelligent or not) God created them. More could be said, but the upshot is that the existence of extraterrestrials (intelligent or otherwise) poses no challenge to the Christian doctrine of creation.

With regard to revelation, one might be concerned that the existence of extraterrestrials poses problems for Christian scriptures and the belief that God has revealed himself to human beings here on Earth at certain times throughout human history. Again, however, this problem is easily dealt with. There is no reason to believe that God's revelatory powers are constrained to Earth alone. If God wanted to, he could reveal his existence to any species, anywhere in the universe. Further, there is nothing about the Christian view of scripture such that an intelligent alien species could not have their own scriptures. These scriptures would never contradict, but might expand upon, our earthly scriptures (subject to proper interpretation, translation, and so on and so forth).

Another possible tension between Christian revelation and the existence of ETIs is simply that there is no mention of life on other planets anywhere in the Bible. If there is life on other planets then this could be seen as a glaring omission, after all whether or not there are other intelligent species out there is an important question! This might cause us to question the status and authority of the Bible.

However, as McIntosh and McNabb point out: 'The reality is that the Christian scriptures are chiefly about God's relationship to man. At the risk of taking a popular analogy too far, it would be odd, to say the least, for a man to mention that there have been others in a love letter to his wife. That is a conversation for a different time and forum. Scripture's silence on the matter should therefore be expected' (2021: 105). We can conclude, therefore, that the silence of scripture on the topic of extraterrestrial life is hardly surprising. It simply wasn't relevant to the writers of the Bible, and there is no reason to assume that God would want a discussion of life on other planets to be included in the various biblical texts, and so the absence of such a discussion should hardly surprise us.

The final category, that of redemption and within this incarnation and salvation, seems to pose a more serious challenge. The difficulty for the Christian is that, according to Christianity, the second person of the Trinity took upon himself a human nature becoming incarnate in the terrestrial human being Jesus of Nazareth here on Earth. Further, it is through participating in his death and resurrection that we are able to achieve salvation. The precise way in which this works is a hotly debated topic with many different perspectives held, but the details do not matter for our purposes (for an overview, see Schmiechen 2005). What matters is that these were earthly events involving God and terrestrial human beings.

The problem now becomes clear: given that terrestrial human beings are saved through participation in these earthly events and processes, how are extraterrestrials saved (if indeed they are)? Do they also need to partake in these earthly events and processes? If so, given they aren't here on Earth, how do they do this? If not, how are they saved? And so on. The answer to these and other closely related questions is far from clear and thus these problems seem to pose a more significant challenge to traditional Christian belief.

Before attempting to put forward some solutions to these questions, it is worth examining historical answers to these and other similar sorts of questions to see how these might inform our answer today. Therefore, it is to historical perspectives that we now turn, before returning to the question of redemption at the end of this section.

Two Historical Views

One might assume that these questions have only begun to concern Christians in the last hundred years or so as a result of our increased knowledge of the size of the universe and thus of the possibility of alien life within it. However, theologians have been wrestling with questions like these for a very long time. For early and medieval Christians, the world was largely unexplored leaving room for the possibility that large swathes of it were inhabited by monstrous, almost-human creatures. As a result, the very same questions which concern modern-day Christians when considering the possibility of intelligent extraterrestrials, also concerned early and medieval Christians when considering the possible existence of earthly, almost-human creatures. A full overview of the differing answers given by theologians throughout history would take us beyond the space available. However, two particularly illuminating highlights can be offered:

Ratramnus (800–868 AD) was a Frankish monk from the monastery of Corbie near Amiens in what is now northern France. He is best known for his writings on the Eucharist and on predestination, but another remarkable text of his survives which discusses the theological status of the *cynocephali*, monstrous dog-headed men rumoured to have lived in the far north. The text appears to have been part of a lengthier exchange (now lost) between him and a priest named Rimbert (c. 830–888 AD) who engaged in regular missionary activity in what is now Denmark and Scandinavia. This suggests that the exchange, initiated by Rimbert, was more than an exercise in idle speculation and that he may have been genuinely considering what steps would be most appropriate should he meet these dog-headed men (Bruce 2006: 46).

Ratramnus appears to have taken the question of the cynocephali seriously. After carefully consulting his monastery's rich library, whilst encouraging Rimbert to also gather as much information as possible, Ratramnus came to the conclusion that such creatures would in fact be human beings, in possession of a soul, and thus suitable for evangelization and salvation. This conclusion differed markedly from the views of various distinguished predecessors, with whom Ratramnus appears to have been familiar, including no less an authority than St Augustine of Hippo (354–430 AD) (Bruce 2006: 55). However, as we shall see, their disagreement did not concern underlying principles, rather it concerned (putative) empirical differences on the facts of the matter.

Ratramnus's argument is simple. Following Augustine, he believed that what makes us human is our rationality, not our physical appearance (Matter 2006: 46–7). Augustine believed that speech is a key marker of rationality and, based on the sources available to him at the time, he believed that the cynocephali did not possess the powers of speech, instead communicating solely through animal barking. On the basis of this, Augustine believed that the cynocephali were not rational, thus not human, and therefore that they had no part in God's plan for human salvation (Bruce 2006: 49). Ratramnus, however, based both on Rimbert's report of the culture of the cynocephali (supposedly they lived in villages, covered their private parts, had domesticated animals, etc.), and based on the legend of the dog-headed Saint Christopher, concluded that the cyno-cephali are in fact human beings, despite their monstrous appearance (Bruce 2006: 52–3; Matter 2006: 52–3). Therefore, according to Ratramnus, they have a part in God's plan for human salvation and are appropriate targets of evangelization.

We could go into further detail, but one key conclusion we can draw from this is that going all the way back to Augustine in the fourth and fifth centuries we have Christian thinkers considering the theological implications of, what we might call, 'exotic' human beings, that is, rational animals whose appearance differs greatly from ours. Further, by the ninth century we have at least one respected theological thinker considering this possibility in a positive and inclusive manner. At the same time, one thing to observe is that both Augustine and Ratramnus held that any 'exotic' human beings would have to have been descended ultimately from the biblical Adam in order to be con-sidered human since it is from our parents that we derive our essence and thus our humanity (Matter 2006: 47, 52; Bruce 2006: 55). As a result, their argu-ments could not be directly applied to extraterrestrials without us making certain other theological assumptions or modifications.

(For the interested reader, a translation of *Ratramnus's Epistola de Cynocephalis* can be found in Dutton (2004: 452–5). Saint Augustine's discussion of the cynocephali can be found in *Concerning the City of God against the Pagans*, Book XVI, Chapter 8. There are many translations. A recent example includes *The City of God*, translated by William Babcock with notes by Boniface Ramsey (2012).)

The fifteenth-century philosopher, theologian, and cardinal Nicholas of Cusa (1401–1464 AD) shared in Ratramnus's openness to the possibility of exotic, created, physical intelligences. Remarkably, Nicholas explicitly considered the possibility, and affirmed the reality, of alien life. In his book *On Learned Ignorance*, he writes:

> We surmise, that in the solar region there are inhabitants which are more solar, brilliant, illustrious, and intellectual – being even more spiritlike than [those] on the moon, where [the inhabitants] are more moonlike than [those] on the earth, [where they are] more material and more solidified … We believe this on the basis of the fiery influence of the sun and on the basis of the watery and aerial influence of the moon and the weighty material influence of the earth. In like manner, we surmise that none of the other regions of the stars are empty of inhabitants – as if there were as many particular mondial parts of the one universe as there are stars, of which there is no number. (quoted in Foltz 2019: 360)

Whilst this was by no means a commonly held view within Christianity at this time, the breadth of Nicholas's vision of a universe teeming with life, all with a role in God's plan for creation, is striking. Further, his assertion that these ETIs are likely more 'solar, brilliant, illustrious, and intellectual' than us regular humans here on Earth repudiates any accusation that Christianity by its very nature must be both theologically geocentric and anthropocentric. More importantly for our purposes, however, we can again see that Christian thinkers have long wrestled with the possibilities raised by the existence of created, physical intelligences, like us in some ways, but very unlike us in others.

Sinless Aliens?

We have seen that Christians throughout history have wrestled with questions sometimes not dissimilar, and sometimes identical, to the ones that concern this section. As a result, the question now becomes: how might Christians today accommodate the possibility of intelligent extraterrestrial life, particularly with regard to incarnation and salvation as detailed earlier? What options are available to Christians here?

One option, perhaps hinted at by Nicholas of Cusa when he writes of 'inhabitants which are more solar, brilliant, illustrious, and intellectual – being even more spiritlike' (quoted in Foltz 2019: 360), is that these potential extraterrestrials are in fact sinless, and thus have need neither of salvation nor a saviour; they may advance directly to heaven. This option has been explored at great length in the fictional work of C. S. Lewis in his Cosmic Trilogy. In the first of that series, *Out of the Silent Planet* (1938), these themes are examined most explicitly. Without going into too much detail, in it the protagonist, Dr. Elwin Ransom, is kidnapped and transported to 'Malachandra' (which we later discover is the planet Mars). Throughout the course of the story Ransom spends some time living with various Malachandrians and soon discovers that sin is 'alien' (forgive the pun!) to these creatures. He finds himself baffled by their inability to grasp why one would want to sin, and they in turn are bemused and often horrified by his descriptions of our sinful behaviour here on Earth. More could be said, and the interested reader is encouraged to read Lewis's series for themselves, but the point for our purposes is that because these creatures have not sinned, they do not need an incarnated saviour. As a result, the issues listed earlier simply do not apply to these sinless creatures. Returning to the questions listed earlier, do these creatures need to partake in God's earthly incarnation, death and resurrection? No. How then are they saved? Through a combination of God's grace and their own sinless nature. Of course, this is only a very rough sketch of how it might work, and further detail would be needed before we would have a fully satisfactory answer, but this overview will suffice for our purposes. The point is that if these creatures are sinless, we can sketch out a coherent account for how they could fit into God's plan for salvation.

Surprisingly, a close contemporary of Nicholas of Cusa, the French theologian and philosopher William Vorilong (ca. 1390–1463), also wrote on the possibility of ETIs and, after arguing that God could have created many inhabited worlds, proposes this exact same solution: 'If it be inquired whether men exist on that world, and whether they have sinned as Adam sinned, I answer no, for they would not exist in sin and did not spring from Adam' (quoted in McColley and Miller 1937: 388). Given that he links sin with being a descendant of Adam, Vorilung's argument seems to rely on a robust conception of inherited original sin, which some modern-day thinkers may shy away from, nevertheless it is remarkable to see a medieval philosopher and theologian considering such a forward thinking and cosmically optimistic possibility so long ago.

One obvious objection that someone might raise here is that, according to the Apostle Paul, 'all have sinned and fall short of the glory of God' (Romans 3:23). If taken at face value this would seem to imply that any potential extraterrestrials must also have sinned and would therefore be in need of a saviour just like we are. Therefore, the option just considered (that they are sinless) is unavailable to Christians.

However, this is all too hasty, and we need not apply Romans 3:23 in this excessively universal manner. For a start, according to mainstream Christianity, there must be at least one exception, namely the person of Jesus Christ (1 John 3:5). Further, according to St Thomas Aquinas (non-fallen) angels have also never sinned (ST I, Q. 62, Art. 8) and various other theologians have followed him in this belief. Additionally, Catholics hold that Mary was sinless (Catholic Church 1997: paras 490–5), and reason itself would seem to indicate that those who die before attaining reason, such as those who die in the womb or in infancy, or who never attain reason, perhaps due to a severe learning disability, never commit sin. After all, these people are neither aware of the (potential) wrongness of their actions nor are they fully in control of them. Thus, reason would seem to suggest that they are innocent in a way those of us who have attained reason, are aware of our actions and their potential wrongness, and are fully in control of our behaviour, and yet who still choose to sin are not. As Scott Hahn points out, rather than claiming that literally everyone has sinned, instead:

> Paul is arguing against the Judaizers by showing them, from several Old Testament passages, that it wasn't only gentiles who were under sin's power but many Jews, too. The Greek word translated as 'all' (*pas*) is used in a distributive sense, meaning many gentiles and many Jews. It does not mean 'everyone without exception'. (2007: 109)

This allows for the possibility that there are sinless intelligent aliens somewhere in the universe, and thus this option remains a viable one for Christians.

Godforsaken Aliens

Let us assume, however, that these potential intelligent extraterrestrials have, like us, sinned after all. What options are available to Christians then?

One theoretical option is that God has simply abandoned them to their sin and that there is no hope for their salvation. This view, as distasteful as it should strike us, is logically coherent. God is not obliged to save anyone. Therefore, God does no wrong in abandoning an intelligent alien species to their sin and not saving them. The obvious objection that one might raise here is that given God has provided us earthly human beings with a route to salvation, why has he not done this for this (potential) alien species? After all, it would seem to be unfair to save one species, but not another.

To this, there are two or three possible responses. First, God is not obliged to be fair. God is not obliged to do anything. Therefore, if God wants to be unfair, that is his prerogative. (One can imagine a Calvinist theologian, say, making this response.) Second, perhaps there is a morally relevant distinction between us and them such that it is not unfair for God to save us, but not to save this (potential) alien species. For example, it is conceptually possible that this alien species is vastly more evil and sinful than we are. Perhaps, rather than being the worst sentient species in the universe from a moral perspective (as per the first option, with unfallen, sinless aliens) we are the best sentient species in the universe from a moral perspective! This is not to say that human beings would therefore be deserving of salvation – since no one is righteous, not even one (Romans 3:10) – rather it would simply be to say that whilst we are fallen and sinful, we are *less* fallen and sinful than the various other sentient species in the universe. This option is conceptually possible, and if this was the case then perhaps it would be perfectly fair for God to save us whilst abandoning a far more sinful alien species to its fate. This idea, it seems to us, is conceptually coherent.

These two responses could be bolstered with the observation that it is often held that there is no hope of salvation for demons. (See, e.g., Aquinas ST I, Q. 64, Art. 2.) If these creatures have no hope of salvation, and God does no wrong in leaving them to this fate, then perhaps it could be argued that there is nothing theologically offensive in the idea that God has abandoned sinful ETIs to their fate.

Despite the fact that this option is conceptually coherent, we should perhaps reject it for two main reasons. First, to assume that we are morally the best species in the universe would be arrogance of the highest order, and thus we should work on the assumption that any intelligent alien species, should they exist, are no worse than us from a moral perspective, and that it is entirely possible that they may be our moral superiors. Second, whilst it is conceptually possible that God might arbitrarily favour us over other intelligent alien species, it would seem, to borrow a scholastic phrase, 'unfitting' for God to create a species with the same fundamental nature as us (that of rational animality) but to abandon them (and not us) to their fate. God is merciful, and whilst he may be morally permitted to create such a species, it would hardly seem merciful to abandon them in this way.

With regard to the fact that God has, so to speak, abandoned demons to their fate, it is worth noting that not all theologians have held this, and those who do believe that the reason there is no hope for these fallen angels is not primarily due to any unwillingness on God's part to save them, but instead it is because of their inability to turn from their sinful ways and towards God. It is often held that angels cannot change their minds once they have committed to a course of action, for example, because they have 'inflexible' freewill. This simply means that although angels have freewill and can make free choices, once those choices have been made, they cannot change their minds, unlike us human beings. To fully explain why certain theologians have held this would lead us too far afield, but, very briefly, the freewill of angels is thought to be inflexible due to their immaterial and more perfect nature lacking potentiality, and thus the potential to change their mind. (See Aquinas ST I, Q. 63, Art. 6 and Q. 64, Art. 2 for a more detailed discussion of these issues.)

As a result, if there are any intelligent extraterrestrials then their freewill will have to be flexible in the same way that our freewill is flexible because of their material and (when compared to the angels) less perfect nature. Thus, fallen angels (demons) fail to act as a suitable precedent for God abandoning a species of sinful intelligent extraterrestrials to their fate.

For these reasons, whilst it is logically possible for there to exist an extraterrestrial species which has been abandoned by God to their sinful ways with no hope of salvation, it is perhaps not the most attractive option for the Christian theologian. Other options will have to be considered.

If we reject the previous options, then two plausible options remain for us to consider. The first is that Christ has only incarnated once, here on Earth, as a terrestrial human being, and that all intelligent species (terrestrial or otherwise) can achieve salvation through participation in this earthly incarnation. The second is that there have been multiple incarnations with Christ incarnating himself once for every alien species out there.

Sinful Aliens: One Incarnation to Save Them All

Let us begin with the first option, namely that Christ has only incarnated once, here on Earth, as a terrestrial human being, and that all intelligent species (terrestrial or otherwise) can achieve salvation through participation in this earthly incarnation. This option allows for the possibility of alien salvation without having to postulate sinless aliens, so it looks like it does what we need it to do.

However, two objections might occur to the reader at this juncture. First, many see the incarnation of the second person of the Trinity as 'the taking of manhood into God' (Polkinghorne 1989: 90). Crucially, however, God had to become a human being like us here on Earth in order to make us 'partakers of the divine nature' (1 Peter 2.14):

> 'For this is why the Word became man, and the Son of God became the Son of man: so that man, by entering into communion with the Word and thus receiving divine sonship, might become a son of God.'; 'For the Son of God became man so that we might become God.'; 'The only-begotten Son of God, wanting to make us sharers in his divinity, assumed our nature, so that he, made man, might make men gods.' (Catholic Church 1997: para. 460, quoting Sts Irenaeus, Athanasius and Thomas Aquinas, respectively)

Therefore, some might argue, these aliens, given they are not members of *Homo sapiens*, cannot partake in the incarnation (including Jesus's death and resurrection) in the way that we earthly human beings can.

This objection, however, need not concern us. As we have seen, there is a long theological and philosophical tradition of seeing our humanity as being tied not to the specific details of our physical appearance, but instead to our nature as rational animals. Intelligent extraterrestrials, if they exist, will share in our nature as rational animals and therefore if God has assumed 'humanity' in this manner, then their nature will also have been taken into God in this way.

Additionally, from a biblical perspective, as we have seen, there is nothing about the creation narrative in Genesis to rule out the possibility that God could have created other intelligent creatures on other planets. Further, they too could be made in the 'image of God' (*imago dei*), since it is usually held that being made in the image of God concerns our intellectual and moral faculties, rather than our physical appearance (see, e.g., O'Neill 2018). Therefore, if these potential aliens are intelligent then they too would be made in the image of God. As Losch and Krebs explain:

> Furthermore, extraterrestrial beings could reflect God's image as well. Not only 'the first man,' but any man is called 'Adam,' as the name is taken from 'adamah,' which means soil. So man is actually a 'soiling' or 'dustling' with a God-given breath and life, as the second creation narrative tells us. There may well be other 'dustlings' on other planets that are equally created in the image and inspired by the breath of God. Being created in the image of God means being a responsible steward for the habitable world. (Losch and Krebs 2015: 236)

We can see these sorts of assumptions reflected in the work of Ratramnus, as explained earlier. He was unconcerned, per se, by the unusual appearance of the dog-headed men and clearly thought that Christ could be their saviour as easily as he could be ours. He saw no need to postulate a 'dog-headed Jesus' who would need to die for these dog-headed men. Rather, he clearly felt that Christ's humanity was such that it could also apply to these dog-headed men. Christ's humanity, regardless of the finer details of how we conceive of it, is suitably flexible so as to allow him to be the saviour of both 'exotic' (be they dog-headed or extraterrestrial) and 'regular' human beings.

The second objection to this option is epistemic in nature, namely, how would these aliens know about the Jesus's incarnation, death and resurrection in order to accept his sacrifice? This objection is easily dealt with. Given God's ability to transmit information to human beings through prophecy as evidenced throughout the scriptures, we can be confident God would find a way to share whatever information is necessary for their salvation (if any is necessary) with these aliens. Their situation would then be more-or-less similar to those human beings who lived either before Christ, or who lived after him, but before 'first contact' with the Christian missionaries (for overviews, see Sullivan 1992; Bullivant 2011).

Therefore, it seems that even if there are sinful intelligent aliens out there, we can coherently hold that there has only been one incarnation here on Earth, and that this incarnation is sufficient to save not only us, but however many intelligent alien species there might be out there. This seems to have been the favoured option of the previously mentioned William Vorilong. He writes 'As to the question whether Christ by dying on this earth could redeem the inhabitants of another world, I answer that he is able to do this even if the worlds were infinite, but it would not be fitting for Him to go unto another world that he must die again' (quoted in McColley and Miller 1937: 388). As a result, we can add that, as well as being intellectually coherent, this option also has some historical pedigree. This surely counts in its favour.

Sinful Aliens: Multiple Incarnations

We now turn to the second plausible option if these (potential) aliens have also sinned like we have, namely that there have been multiple incarnations, one for every alien species out there. There are many reasons why we might be drawn to this option. For example, like the previous option, it allows for the possibility of sinful aliens whilst also providing an easy explanation for how they could know about the incarnation of God into their species. Additionally, unlike the previous option, this solution avoids us having to make earthly human beings special in some way. After all, according to the previous option, of all the sentient intelligent species in the universe, God chose to incarnate himself into only one 'human-like' species, ours here on Earth. What is so special about us? This solution, however, allows God to treat all species equally dying for each and every one of them individually.

This is the option adopted by the physicist and theologian John Polkinghorne (1930–2021) who held that 'if there are other forms of self-conscious life in the universe, equally in need of redemption as humankind has proved to be' then we can suppose 'that the Second Person of the Trinity would, in his temporal pole, have taken upon himself their nature, and drawn that nature into Godhead in an act of redemption, thus finding a partial embodiment in them also' (Polkinghorne 1989: 91).

An obvious objection that might be raised here is that according to Romans 6:10: 'The death he [Christ] died, he died to sin once for all; but the life he lives, he lives to God', and according to 1 Peter 3:18: 'For Christ also suffered once for sins, the righteous for the unrighteous, to bring you to God. He was put to death in the body but made alive in the Spirit'. These passages would seem to indicate that Jesus's death and resurrection was a one-time event and therefore he could not go through the same process for other alien species.

There are two responses we could make to this. First, very simply, we could argue that the collection of scriptures that make up 'our' Bible were written *by* human beings (inspired by the Holy Spirit) *for* human beings here on Earth. We can assume, therefore, that the Biblical writers were only thinking of earthly incarnations and that therefore their emphasis on the one-time nature of Jesus's death and resurrection is solely terrestrial in scope. The incarnation, and Jesus's death and resurrection, has only happened and will only happen once here on Earth, but this allows for the possibility that similar events could take place on other planets for other species.

The second response we could make is that is that the event of Christ's incarnation, death, and resurrection is one of many parts, with those parts taking place throughout the universe and throughout time. This idea should not strike us as strange. There is nothing incoherent about holding that WW2 was a single event which took place across an extended period of time (1939–1945) and which was made up of many different parts which were events in their own right, for example the D-Day landings on 6th June 1944. Likewise, we might coherently hold that Christ's incarnation is a single event, consisting of many different parts scattered across time and throughout the universe. In this way, the unique event of the incarnation could take place in such a manner as to allow God to take into himself not only earthly human beings, but all intelligent species, and perhaps even (indirectly) the whole universe. As Polkinghorne explains:

> The more seriously one takes the divinity of Christ, the more seriously one must wrestle with the notion that the hypostatic union of his two natures [that Christ was fully man and fully God] must involve something like the way in which an infinite-dimensional sphere would intersect a two-dimensional plane in the perfect symmetry of a circle. Then, if on other planets there are other created natures united to the Word, that would involve other 'sections' of the Divine sphere. (Polkinghorne 1989: 91)

We can conclude, therefore, that if there are sinful aliens then there is nothing incoherent about holding that there have been multiple incarnations to allow for their redemption and salvation.

Narrative Conflict?

McIntosh and McNabb (2021), after discussing many of the issues examined in this section, consider another potential challenge to Christianity should intelligent extraterrestrials exist, namely, that of narrative conflict. Such a challenge is by no means a disproof of Christianity, but it does perhaps render it less plausible or believable. Imagine you are watching a film at the cinema.

Let's imagine it is a romantic comedy and that it has been widely commended by both your friends and film critics. You are approaching the 90-minute mark. The protagonists, after various hilarious mishaps and false starts, have fallen in love, but do not realise their love is mutually reciprocated. The female protagonist believing her love is unrequited finds it too painful living so near to the male protagonist. She leaves her home and heads to the airport to start a new life elsewhere. The male protagonist asks her neighbour where she is and realises, based on her neighbour's comments, that she also loves him, so he rushes to the airport to stop her. A dramatic scene ensues in which he runs through security. He reaches her just as she is boarding the plane. They profess their mutual love. They lean in to kiss each other, and just at that moment a UFO blows up the airport (and the White House) killing both of them.

Such a film is not inconceivable, nor is it logically incoherent, but there is something jarring about such a narrative. It would appear that two very different films have somehow mistakenly been spliced together. In a similar way, the Christian worldview involves a narrative. Different Christians will articulate this narrative in different ways, but certainly God's love for mankind (John 3:16) and our response to that love are key components. The Christian story, then, could be described as a love story or a romance. (Whether it is a romantic *comedy*, we'll leave to the reader!)

In the same way that the alien invasion created a degree of narrative tension in our romantic comedy as explained earlier, the existence of aliens therefore might also create a degree of narrative tension for Christianity, and this might count against its plausibility and believability. McIntosh and McNabb (2021) consider this exact objection. They begin by pointing out that how much narrative tension the existence of aliens might raise depends upon the circumstances of their existence and (potential) interactions with us. They consider five different scenarios:

S1. ETI is so remote or undetectable that any interaction is (nomologically) impossible.

S2. ETI is so remote as to be physically inaccessible, but communication is possible.

S3. Physical interaction with ETI is possible; ETI is peaceable.

S4. Physical interaction with ETI is possible; ETI is hostile but not an existential threat.

S5. Physical interaction with ETI is possible; ETI is hostile and an existential threat. (McIntosh and McNabb 2021: 14)

They point out that S1 does very little to the Christian narrative. Extraterrestrial intelligences would remain forever an abstract and unverifiable possibility, and thus little more than an intellectual puzzle as examined in this section (and in McIntosh and McNabb's paper, and so on).

They then point out that S2 and S3 could raise some degree of tension. At the very least, the questions considered in this section would become 'live', and others might emerge. At the same time, we would point out that the opposite might be the case. If rather than coming 'in peace', aliens came 'in the name of the Father, and of the Son, and of the Holy Spirit' with fresh theological insights, a set of scriptures to complement our own, and so on, then this would seem to strengthen and enlarge the Christian narrative, rather than threatening it.

That said, as McIntosh and McNabb point out, S4 and S5 both seem to create more serious narrative tension. They respond to this challenging by suggesting the need for a 'hostile ETI theodicy' which would attempt to reconcile the existence of hostile extraterrestrials with a Christian worldview and narrative. They then explore three works of fiction which explore S4 and S5 scenarios, each of which have, if not explicit Christian themes, at least Christian (and theistic) sympathies. Very briefly, they point out that in the film *Signs*, written and directed by M. Night Shyamalan and starring Mel Gibson, the protagonist, an ex-priest turned farmer, is struggling with various doubts and burdens. His faith is wavering after the loss of his wife in a car accident, and he struggles to manage his son's poor physical, and his daughter's poor mental, health. Eventually, however, these burdens come together in a providential manner so as to allow them all to survive an alien invasion, thus restoring his faith in God and instigating his return to the priesthood. Thus, a Christian narrative can be identified even in the context of an alien invasion. They then point out that in Orson Scott Card's *Ender's Game* book series. The protagonist, Ender, defeats an alien race by learning to empathise with them so much he begins to love them. After defeating them, he then becomes something of a cosmic priest, acting as an envoy between both humans and aliens, but also the aliens and God, thus bringing about some degree of reconciliation and healing. Whilst the first example involved a more personal Christian narrative, for the priest and his family, this second example has a more cosmic scale. Finally, they examine Mary Doria Russell's *The Sparrow*, where a group of Jesuit missionaries attempt to make contact with an alien species. All but one of the missionaries is killed, many of them by the aliens themselves. The remaining missionary returns home and spends the rest of his life trying to make sense of it all, growing closer to God as a result. This narrative, whilst more ambiguous than the previous two, perhaps because of its very ambiguity possibly more closely matches our own experiences. Life is ambiguous, and there is no reason to suppose alien life is any different.

McIntosh and McNabb go on to examine these issues in a little more detail, but hopefully this brief summary will suffice for our purposes. The only thing we would add to McIntosh and McNabb's discussion is that the Christian story is one of subverted expectations and narrative tensions. For example, God forms a covenant with a chosen people, only to leave them languishing in Egypt in slavery for hundreds of years. He then brings them out of Egypt and establishes a home for them. Whereupon they turn to other gods, causing God himself to abandon all but a remnant. This remnant then waits for the Messiah. Many of them expect him to be a political and military leader who will overthrow their enemies. Instead, when the Messiah comes, he is a carpenter and itinerant preacher who dies on a cross. His enemies believe that this is the end of the matter, only for him to come back to life after three days! We could go on, but the point is clear. The Christian story is one of subverted expectations and narrative tension. Therefore, Christians should not fear the possibility of narrative tension should we discover intelligent alien life in the future. If Christianity is correct, such tension will be reconciled in the long run, and when it is a more complete and glorious picture will emerge.

Conclusion

For Thomas Paine, 'to believe that God created a plurality of worlds, at least as numerous as what we call stars, renders the Christian system of faith at once little and ridiculous, and scatters it in the mind like feathers in the air' (1794: 84). If the arguments of this section have been successful, then it should now be clear that this is anything but the case. Whilst the (possible) existence of ETIs raises a number of complex questions for Christianity, there are numerous possible answers that could be given by way of response. The main problem, as we have seen, is how these extraterrestrials might fit into Christian beliefs about incarnation, redemption and salvation. Several answers have been considered. First, these aliens might be sinless. They could then be saved through a combination of their own sinlessness and God's mercy. There would then be no need for God to incarnate himself for them and their salvation. Second, it is logically possible that these aliens have sinned, but that God has simply abandoned them to their fate. Whilst this is logically possible, it seems highly unlikely given God's merciful and loving nature, and so we can reject this option as too implausible to take seriously. Third, if these aliens have sinned then it is possible that Christ's incarnation here on Earth is efficacious for their salvation as well as ours. This is because, whilst perhaps looking very different to us, any intelligent alien species would share in the same fundamental nature as us human beings here on Earth (namely, rational animality). Therefore, when

God took on a human nature, he would have also taken on alien nature, since they are one and the same. Finally, it is possible that God has incarnated himself multiple times throughout the universe and across time, once for each intelligent alien species. All of these options are possible.

We have also seen that whilst the existence of ETIs might risk creating a degree of narrative tension for a Christian worldview, this tension can be diffused. Whilst we don't yet know how this narrative tension might be created, since we haven't yet discovered aliens and we don't yet know the circumstances of their existence and relationship with us, we have seen through various works of fiction that even an alien invasion can be understood through the lens of a Christian worldview and in the context of a Christian narrative. Thus, once again, the possibility of alien life does little to challenge a Christian worldview.

As a final caveat, it is worth stressing that this section is speculative. Given that God's ways are not our ways (Isaiah 55:8–9), it seems perfectly possible that if there are intelligent aliens out there that they will fit into God's plan for Creation in a way we have not considered, and perhaps in a way that we cannot imagine, at least at present. This is particularly the case if we are prepared to countenance, at least for extraterrestrials if not terrestrial human beings, a version of Christian salvific pluralism. (As an aside, Ray Bradbury's short story 'The Fire Balloons' plays around with this idea; see Bradbury 2008: 145–72.) Perhaps, therefore, all we can firmly conclude at this stage is that should we ever encounter intelligent aliens we will have a lot to learn about them, about ourselves, and about God.

4 Terrestrial Religions and Extraterrestrial Life

The previous section examined the implications of the discovery of intelligent aliens for mainstream Christianity whilst also outlining a number of strategies for how their existence might be accommodated. This section will apply these same questions to a number of the other major world religions: Judaism, Islam, Hinduism, and Buddhism. Whilst ideally an equal amount of space would be dedicated to each religion, due to limits on space we will only be able to examine these religions in a more cursory manner before pointing the interested reader to further resources.

Judaism

In Jewish thought, one of the most pre-eminent theologians to consider the implications of extraterrestrial life for Judaism was Rabbi Norman Lamm (1927–2020), one of whose most influential papers is his 'The Religious Implications of Extraterrestrial Life' (1965). According to Shatz, Lamm's paper 'is a paradigm of

Torah u-Madda' (Shatz 2021: 255). *Torah u-Madda* is simply the idea that the study of the Torah and the study of the secular world, including the sciences, can be mutually enriching. Given the pre-eminence of Lamm's work and of this paper in particular this looks like a good place to start our exploration of Jewish exotheology.

Lamm suggests that there are three challenges posed by possibility of extra-terrestrial life: the uniqueness of man, the uniqueness of the creator, and the relationship between man and God (Lamm 1965: 21). Beginning with the uniqueness of man, Lamm points out that for Judaism, as for Christianity, human beings are made in the 'image of God' and thus are deemed to be valuable (1965: 21). He then asks whether, should there be intelligent life on other planets, possibly of a higher or more intelligent nature, this might impugn or diminish our intrinsic value and significance. He responds to this by pointing out that:

> Whether the idea of 'the divine Image' is interpreted rationalistically as intelligence, or ethically as freedom of the will, or mystically as possessing creative powers, there is nothing in it (i.e., in the Biblical doctrine per se) that insists upon man's singularity. The concept of *imago dei* does not impose a singular and exclusive quality upon all who possess it. All human beings are created in this divine Image, despite the fact that people are born unequal, some with superior endowments and some with a tragic poverty of both talent and opportunity. In the same manner, races of intelligent beings that differ from each other as radically as an idiot from a great genius may both be impressed by the divine Image, by the summons to transcend the merely natural. If the Image of the Absolutely One God can be impressed upon the manifold individuals within the human race, it can be similarly bestowed upon a multitude of races. (1965: 22–3)

At the same time, Lamm acknowledges that there is a tension here. If there are a multitude of intelligent species in the universe, then this does challenge the uniqueness and specialness of human beings. However, as Lamm points out, this tension is acknowledged in the scriptures themselves:

> When I consider your heavens, the work of your fingers, the moon and the stars, which you have set in place, what is mankind that you are mindful of them, human beings that you care for them? You have made them a little lower than the angels and crowned them with glory and honor. You made them rulers over the works of your hands; you put everything under their feet. (Psalm 8.3–6 NIV)

As a result, Lamm concludes that this need not perturb the Jewish thinker. There is a sense in which human beings have enormous intrinsic value, and there is another sense in which we are insignificant. If there are other intelligent species out there then this merely reinforces the already acknowledged tension: at a cosmic level human beings are both important and unimportant, relevant and irrelevant, and so on.

Lamm then goes on to highlight that there are two historical perspectives on the uniqueness and importance of man and of his location in the universe. Saadia (892–942) and Maimonides (1138–1204) both believed in a geocentric universe as was the scientific consensus at the time, and yet they interpreted the philosophical and theological implications of this very differently. For Saadia, our location at the centre of the universe demonstrates our unique importance. We are the telos and axle of the universe (Lamm 1965: 25–6). According to Saadia, observation of nature supports this conclusion. Seeds are the most important part of a fruit, and they sit at the centre. Likewise, yolks sit in the centre of their eggs, and, in human beings, our hearts sit in the middle of our chests. Thus, our position at the centre of the universe reflects our unique importance.

Maimonides, however, takes the exact opposite approach. Maimonides (perhaps influenced by Aristotle where Saadia was influenced by Plato) argues that the more noble something is the further from the centre of the universe it will be. To put it very simply, according to Maimonides (and Aristotle) noble things go 'up', since they are more refined, and thus 'out' from the spherical Earth that forms the centre of the universe. Therefore, according to Maimonides, there is nothing special about man. According to Maimonides, human beings are merely 'a drop splashed out of the cosmic bucket' (Lamm 1965: 29).

Lamm, as we read him, describes the views of these thinkers for two reasons. Firstly, to highlight the differing (and opposing) views held within Judaism on the importance of human beings. Secondly, and perhaps more importantly, to demonstrate that we need not attribute any philosophical or theological significance to our geographical location in the universe. Both Saadia and Maimonides did think our location in the universe was significant and yet they came to opposite conclusions. Likewise, whether we are just one species amongst many located on the outskirts of a huge universe teeming with intelligent life, or whether we are truly unique and located right at the centre of a physical universe created just for us tells us nothing about our relative importance. As Lamm explains: 'Similarly, the claim by a race to spiritual dignity and intrinsic metaphysical value does not depend upon a 'good' cosmic address. It depends only upon the ability of the members of that race to enter into a dialogue with the Creator of all races. God makes Himself available to His creatures wherever they are in His immense universe; He is not a social snob who will not be seen in the cosmic slums and alleys' (Lamm 1965: 32).

Lamm then turns to the question of the uniqueness of God as the Creator of life. In particular, the concern he addresses is whether, should human beings find a way to create synthetic life in a lab as part of a quest to understand how life might have evolved through naturalistic processes elsewhere in the universe, this would in some way challenge the importance and uniqueness of God as the Creator of life. Lamm responds to this by pointing out that God will still be the ultimate Creator of all life in the universe even if intermediary agents take part in that process. He gives the biblical example of Solomon who, according to the Bible, was responsible for building the Temple in Jerusalem. Lamm points out that, in a sense, Solomon didn't build the Temple. Rather, his various workers and architects built the Temple based on his commands, and yet the Bible simply says that 'Solomon built the Temple' and other phrases to this effect. Why? Because in the context of this analogy, Solomon was the ultimate cause of the Temple being built, even though there were various intermediaries who actually made it happen. Likewise, even if we create life in a lab, given God is the ultimate Creator of the universe, God will still be the ultimate Creator of that life, with human beings merely acting as intermediaries (Lamm 1965: 39). We think Lamm is right to point this out and would add that even though we have not yet created synthetic life in a lab, to some extent this relationship already holds. Each of us was 'created' by our parents and we may well go on to 'create' children of our own, and yet we still view God as our (ultimate) Creator. It seems, therefore, that this relationship already holds. As a result, if human beings ever do create synthetic life in a lab this will do nothing to challenge the uniqueness of God as the (ultimate) Creator of life.

Finally, Lamm turns to the implications of the existence of intelligent aliens for our relationship with God. He observes that some people might be concerned that:

> If the universe is so much more vast and complex than we heretofore imagined; if man is much less singular, no longer unique, and perhaps surpassed in wisdom by other non-terrestrial species; then perhaps God is so great, so remote, that He is unconcerned with us earth-creatures strutting self-centeredly over an insignificant planet. The very majesty of His universe threatens such fundamentals as God's Providence, His personality, His relatedness to His creatures. To imagine that God has personality, like a mere mortal earth-man; that He is concerned with our trivial interests; that He has anything to do with us – is considered an embarrassment, an offense to our modesty. The threat is not so much intellectual and theological as emotional and psychological; but what begins as the latter often ends as the former. (Lamm 1965: 43)

Lamm responds to this by highlighting that God is both transcendent and immanent and that to emphasize one at the expense of the other is a mistake. Whilst the size and scale of the universe might highlight to us God's transcendence, we must never forget that God is also immanent. As Lamm explains, 'part of God's endless praise is that despite His loftiness and our lowliness, He is still concerned with every one of us – and every other rational sentient race anywhere' (1965: 48) and that 'A God who can exercise providence over one billion earthmen can do so for ten billion times that number of creatures throughout the universe. He is not troubled, one ought grant, by problems in communications, engineering, or the complexities of cosmic cybernetics' (1965: 50).

Lamm's paper is both long and dense, so we have only been able to offer a very brief summary of its key points. However, one issue that does seem conspicuously absent from Lamm's paper is a discussion of the implications of the existence of extraterrestrials for the Jewish people in particular. This might strike us as odd given it is a paper laying out a Jewish exotheology. According to Judaism, the Jewish people are a 'chosen people' (Exodus 19:5, Deuteronomy 7:5–6, 14:2, Amos 3:2). What precisely this amounts to is open to debate, but it is generally agreed that it means that God has a unique covenant with the Jewish people (Genesis 17:7) and that they are to act as a nation of priests (Exodus 19:6). The question now becomes, if there are intelligent aliens on other planets, what implications does this have, if any, for the special relationship between God and the Jewish people? Could there be an 'alien chosen people'? If so, might this undermine the uniqueness of the Jewish people's relationship with God? If not, could these aliens convert to Judaism or are they excluded from this relationship? And so on.

In her paper 'Judaism and Extraterrestrials: Theological Lessons from Science Fiction' (2019), Mara Wendy Cohen Ioannides examines at least one aspect of the previously mentioned problem(s), namely, whether or not aliens could convert to Judaism. After some scene setting, she begins to answer this question by examining what makes someone a Jew. She points out that, fairly obviously, Jews are human beings, and so she first attempts to offer a Jewish definition of a human being. She points out that:

The Talmud, in Chagigah 16, describes six characteristics of humans:

1. In three they are like ministering angels:
   i   They have understanding;
   ii They walk upright;
   iii They speak in the holy language (Hebrew).
2. In three they are like animals:
   i   They eat and drink;
   ii They propagate;
   iii They defecate. (Ioannides 2019: 1205)

Here, as Ioannides acknowledges, we see echoes of Aristotle's definition of man as a rational animal; we are animals, but we are distinctive and one of the ways we are distinctive, according to the Talmud, is in our understanding.

She then notes that more recently Loike and Tendler (2003) have argued that according to Jewish law a human being must possess at least one of the following three characteristics:

1. having been formed within or born from a human,
2. expressing moral intelligence,
3. being capable of producing offspring with a human. (Ioannides 2019: 1206)

Ioannides points out that whilst the first and third will not apply to intelligent extraterrestrials, the second likely could. Once again, like in our previous section, we can see that there is a sense in which intelligent extraterrestrials are 'humans' albeit of a very exotic variety. What matters is not how many arms or legs they have, the colour of their skin, whether they are carbon-based or silicon-based, and so on. What matters is that they are capable of engaging in abstract thought, ethical reasoning, co-operation, and so on. In this sense, intelligent extraterrestrials could be 'one of us'.

Ioannides has now provided us with a Jewish account of human nature. Obviously, not all human beings are Jewish, however, so what is it that makes a human being Jewish? Ioannides explains that: 'According to Jewish law, there are two main ways to become a Jew. One way is to be born of a Jewish parent. All Jewish movements accept matrilineal claims, while the Reform Movement also accepts patrilineal ... The second way is to choose to become a Jew, to convert' (Ioannides 2019: 1204–5). She then points out that the traditional requirement (alluded to in the Talmudic requirements listed earlier) that Jews speak Hebrew is negated since many contemporary Jews speak limited, if any, Hebrew (2019: 1206). Therefore, she concludes that today 'a Jew is a sentient being who can communicate and reason' (2019: 1206–7). Presumably, given she stated it earlier, she also believes that to be Jewish they must either be born of a Jewish mother (or father) or that they must have converted and that she has simply not stated it here explicitly to avoid repetition.

We now have our definition of a Jewish person. The question now becomes: 'Can this definition be applied to extraterrestrials?' (Ioannides 2019: 1207). Ioannides explores this question by examining various examples of Jewish science fiction and, perhaps unsurprisingly, ultimately, she answers in the affirmative: (intelligent) aliens could convert to Judaism.

There is much more that could be said about Jewish exotheology, but we will have to leave our discussion of it here for now. Instead, we now turn to the youngest, and second largest, of the Abrahamic faiths: Islam.

Islam

Given that Islam, like Judaism and Christianity, is a monotheistic Abrahamic faith, much of what has been said previously during our discussion of Jewish and Christian exotheology can be applied in an Islamic context. The obvious exceptions, of course, are those aspects of Jewish and Christian theology that are distinctive of, and unique to, those religions individually, most obviously the idea that the Jewish people are a 'chosen people' and the incarnation of Jesus in Jewish and Christian theology respectively. That said, the more general claims about God as the creator of life, his ability to communicate with his creatures, our relationship with God, and so on and so forth, which we have previously discussed can be reasserted in an Islamic context with relative ease given its shared Abrahamic heritage. Of course, the scriptural texts used to support these claims in an Islamic context will be different (due to their different holy texts: the Qur'an and hadith), but the same general principles can be easily identified. Therefore, to avoid repetition, it is worth focussing on what we shall call Islamic 'distinctives', namely, those aspects of Islam that are unique to Islam and which are of interest to us as exotheologians. It is to these distinctives that we now turn.

Generally speaking, Islam is fairly open to the idea of extraterrestrial life. There is nothing in the Qur'an to rule out the idea that there is life on other planets, and some passages could be seen to be endorsing the idea, for example, one of the names of God ('Allah' in Arabic) is 'Lord of all worlds' (e.g., Qur'an 1:2 and 45:36). Whilst the use of the plural, 'worlds', could be seen to be referring to something like the invisible world of the jinn (to which we shall return) and the visible world of human beings, it could also be interpreted in such a way as to allow for the possibility of, if not to actively endorse the idea that there is, life on other planets. Similarly, the Qur'an states that 'None in the heavens and earth knows the unseen except Allah, and they do not perceive when they will be resurrected' (Qur'an 27:65). Again, the reference to 'the heavens' could be referring to the angels, for example, but it could also be interpreted in such a way as to allow for the possibility of life on other planets whose inhabitants are subject to the same resurrection and judgement as us here on Earth.

Despite this openness, as Malik and Determann have pointed out: 'To date, there are only a handful of publications that discuss Islamic perspectives on IEL [intelligent extraterrestrial life], at least in the English language' (2024). Indeed, other than their own collection of essays, they can cite only four in-depth discussions of Islamic exotheology in English (i.e., Weintraub 2014; Iqbal 2018; Determann 2021; Haider et al. 2023). No doubt there are others in Arabic, Urdu, Bahasa Indonesia, or other languages, but clearly this is an under-researched aspect of Islamic theology. At the same time, this is rapidly changing and there is a growing interest in this topic.

One distinctive aspect of Islamic theology that could aid in their understanding of intelligent alien life and how it might fit into an Islamic worldview is the concept of the jinn. The jinn (from which we derive the English word 'genie') are a class of intelligent creatures like human beings in certain respects, but very different in others. Like human beings, they have freewill and are capable of both good and evil (Qur'an 72.11, etc.). As a result, they, like us, will be judged at the resurrection (Qur'an 7.38, 55.39, 72.13–15, etc.). They also share with us a sexual nature, being both male and female (al-Kisa'I 1978: 19) and needing to reproduce through (something akin to) sex (Ibn 'Arabi 1972: 1: 131–4). They also require sustenance, with their preferred food being bones according to some sources (Ibn 'Arabi 1972: 1:132), and they are both mortal and vulnerable to damage. The jinn are described in the Qur'an as being made of 'scorching fire' (and/or possibly 'scorching wind') (Qur'an 15.27) which suggests that they are not completely immaterial and thus we can add that they share with us finite bodies, albeit of a very different sort. At the same time, the jinn are also very different to us, for example, they are shapeshifters, invisible (when they choose to be) and immensely long-lived. For a more detailed discussion of these issues see Playford (2024), but what we can clearly see is that Islam already believes in an intelligent 'alien' species which is like us in certain respects, but not like us in others. In the same way, if there are intelligent extraterrestrials, they will likely be like us in certain respects, but not in others. This suggests that the jinn could act as a useful model for how Muslims might incorporate ETIs into their worldview.

Whilst the Islamic distinctive of the jinn allows Muslims to more easily accommodate the existence of intelligent aliens into their theology, there are certain Islamic distinctives that create difficulties. Islam, as a religion, is very clearly tied to a particular place and time. For example, all Muslims should perform Hajj, a pilgrimage to the (earthly) city of Mecca at least once in their lives. This hardly seems a reasonable requirement for an intelligent species on a different planet! Likewise, Muslims must pray facing Mecca. This is fairly easy to do if you are here on Earth and you have a compass, but it may well be impossible for an alien species. Similarly, according to Islamic theology, whilst the Qur'an itself exists eternally in Heaven, it was revealed in the seventh century by a particular human being (the Prophet Muhammad) in the Arabian Peninsula. It is therefore written in the Arabic dialect of that time and place. Finally, it also refers to various (earthly) historical events. This raises a number of difficult questions for Muslims. Would these aliens have their own Qur'an written in their own language? If so, is this really *the* Qur'an given its status and importance in Muslim thought? If not, presumably it is written in Arabic. Do these aliens speak Arabic? And so on and so forth. Likewise, we might worry Muhammad's status as the 'Seal of the Prophets' is threatened in some way by the existence of intelligent aliens. Do these aliens have their own prophets? If so, do they have their own final prophet, that is, their own 'Seal of the Prophets'? If so, does that threaten Muhammad's unique status? And so on.

These are difficult questions for Muslims to answer, but it seems likely numerous solutions can be offered in the same way that numerous solutions have been offered to resolve the various questions and difficulties arising out of Jewish and Christian distinctives. It will certainly be interesting to see what solutions are proposed as this aspect of Islamic theology is further developed. Meanwhile, as so often, science fiction authors have been quick to fill the speculative void (Elzembely and Aysha 2021; see Ward 2020 for one entertaining example).

Hinduism

We now turn to the original and largest Dharmic faith: Hinduism. One difficulty that faces us when trying to discuss Hindu exotheology is simply its extreme openness to life on other planets! In a sense, all of Hindu exotheology can be boiled down to the fact that there is nothing about Hinduism that precludes the existence of alien life, and perhaps many aspects of Hinduism that would actively endorse at least the possibility, if not the actuality, of alien life. As a result, it is very difficult to know where to start when tackling this topic.

Up until now, when examining Jewish, Christian and Islamic exotheology, we have primarily focussed on the difficulties ETIs might pose for those faiths and how they might respond. With Hinduism, it might be better to start by examining why the possible reality of such beings poses so few problems. It is to this question, then, that we now turn.

Hindu cosmology is mind-bogglingly vast and ancient (Krishnamurthy 2019: chap. 20). Not only is our universe vast, but there are a vast number of universes (Bhagavata Purana 6.16.37, 10.87.41, 3.11.41; Yoga Vasistha 3.30.16–17). Further, it is explicitly stated in various Hindu texts that life exists on other planets (Yoga Vasistha 3.30.34) and other universes (Garga Samhita 1.2.28). It is hardly surprising, then, that Hindus are very open to the idea of life on other planets.

In addition to this, alien-like creatures are described in various Hindu texts (Manuaba and Sudirman 2018), as are *vimānas*, strange flying machines that sounds remarkably like UFOs (Shivanandam 2015; see Section 6). As a result, not only are many Hindus open to the possibility of alien life, but many are open to the possibility of extraterrestrial visitations, that is, UFOs.

We suspect there are a few other factors we can point to that explains the Hindu openness to extraterrestrial life. Hinduism is a non-anthropocentric religion. According to Hinduism, all living creatures possess souls (as well as bodies). After we die, we can be reincarnated as animals as well as human beings based on whether we have cultivated good or bad karma (Desai 2003). When this is combined with the Hindu doctrine that the goal of existence is to achieve enlightenment, It becomes clear that human beings are both special and not special.

Human beings are special because of our intellect. Unlike animals, human beings can consciously develop good karma, and thus move closer to, and perhaps achieve, enlightenment (Mahābhārata 12.286.31–32). At the same time, if we fail to achieve good karma we can expect to be reincarnated as an animal and it may take many lifetimes until we are given another opportunity to achieve enlightenment. Likewise, whilst an animal does not face the possibility of enlightenment in this lifetime, in future lifetimes they may well get the opportunity. Therefore, we can see that the gap between human beings and animals in Hindu thought is far less than in the Abrahamic traditions. It follows that Hindu anthropology is perhaps less threatened by the idea of alien life than Abrahamic anthropology because, in a sense, there is nothing special about human beings.

In addition to this Hinduism is naturally pluralistic in its outlook and flexible in its theology with numerous pluralistic sentiments present in its holy texts (Rig Veda 1.164.46, Uddhava Gita 3:21, Bhagavad Gita 18:22 and 4:11). This theological flexibility may well also contribute to the Hindu openness to extraterrestrial life.

More could be said, but due to limits on space we will have to leave our discussion of Hinduism here. We now turn to the second largest Dharmic faiths and another of the major world religions: Buddhism.

Buddhism

Buddhism emerged out of a Hindu context some time around the fifth century BC. As a result, it stands in a similar relationship to Hinduism as Christianity and Islam do to Judaism. It should come as no surprise, therefore, to observe that many of the concepts and themes identifiable in Hindu thought can also be identified in Buddhist thought. Restricting our attention to those doctrines of exotheological importance, Buddhists also believe in an ancient if not eternal universe often couched in cyclical language which is highly suggestive of contemporary oscillating models of the universe (Sheth 2004: 6–7). The universe is also vast and filled with planets (Yamamoto and Kuwahara 2008; Wickramasinghe 2014), many of which are teeming with life (Sheth 2004: 7). See, for example, the *Avatamsaka Sutra* (Cleary 1993).

Further, as with Hinduism, Buddhism believes in reincarnation (often called rebirth in a Buddhist context due to their differing metaphysics), thus promoting a non-anthropocentric worldview. Thus, we can clearly see why Buddhism is comparably open to alien life as is Hinduism. Once again, more could be said about the shared exotheological doctrines of Hinduism and Buddhism, but we are keen to avoid excess repetition, so we will now examine a Buddhist distinctive that opens it up to the possibility of extraterrestrial life.

One key Buddhist doctrine is that of 'interdependence'. According to this doctrine, all things are, as the name would imply, interdependent. However, this claim is much more radical than it may at first appear. The Buddhist doctrine of interdependence is not simply the claim that we rely on others for our survival, but that everything, everywhere, depends on other things not only for their existence, but even for their very properties and characteristics. One way to illustrate this would be with the example of colour properties. We might think, for example, that for an object to be red is for that object to be seen as red by certain observers under certain circumstances. (Whether we should understand colour properties in this way is another matter, but the example is illustrative for our purposes.) If this way of understanding colour is correct, then we might conclude that nothing is really coloured in and of itself, rather, an object's colour properties depend on outside observers in order for them to be fully manifest. (Again, we might not have to draw this conclusion, but hopefully this illustrates the idea of interdependence.) As Thuan explains:

> One of the aspects of that interdependence is the relationship between humanity's consciousness and the reality we perceive around us. According to Buddhism, all the proprieties that we attribute to the phenomenal world are not necessarily intrinsic to the object itself, but are conceived by our mind and filtered through our perceptions. Thus the same reality may appear differently to different intelligences. Objects are thus devoid of intrinsic and autonomous properties and do not possess solidity and permanence. That is the profound meaning of 'vacuity.' It must be emphasized that vacuity in Buddhism is not nothingness as the word has sometimes been misunderstood ... Because of interdependence, there is the potential and capacity for phenomena to vary in an infinite number of ways, to develop in infinite directions. The only real nature of phenomena is thus their 'interdependence.' Vacuity is the ultimate nature of things because phenomena are devoid of an existence that is permanent and independent of the observer. (Thuan 2001: 207–8)

This doctrine, when applied in a cosmological context, has profound implications. For a start, it rules out the possibility of a permanent and necessarily existing creator God, that is, the God of classical theism, because such a being would not be interdependent. It also means that the universe, in some form or other, must have always existed, since it can't have emerged from nothing by itself.

(Strictly speaking, one could be a classical theist whilst also believing in interdependence and impermanence. Classical theists, for various technical reasons, do not think of God as a 'thing' amongst other things. Therefore, one could hold to the doctrines of interdependence and impermanence as applied to all 'things' whilst also believing in the classical God of theism since these doctrines simply would not apply to him. Such a view, however, whilst in accordance with the letter of Buddhism, perhaps goes against its spirit, so to speak.)

We can go still further. One thing that has increasingly surprised physicists in recent years is the so-called fine-tuning of the universe for the emergence of life. As Thuan explains:

> Astrophysics teaches us that the emergence of life from the primordial soup depended on an extremely delicate adjustment of the laws of Nature and the initial conditions of the universe. A minute change in the intensity of the fundamental forces, and we would not be around to talk about it. The stars would not have formed and started their marvellous nuclear alchemy. None of the heavy elements that constitute the basis of life would have seen the light of day. The precision of the fine-tuning of the physical constants and of the initial conditions is astonishing. It is similar to the precision that a marksman has to exercise in order to put a bullet through a square target of 1 cm on a side located at the edge of the observable universe some 15 billion light-years away. (Thuan 2001: 212)

How best to explain this fine-tuning is a contentious issue with different thinkers approaching the problem in different ways, but Buddhism has its own answer. Given life and consciousness seem to be interlinked, it appears we have (at least) two fundamental realities: matter and consciousness. If the Buddhist doctrine of interdependence is correct, then consciousness and matter must be interdependent. We now have an explanation for why the universe (matter) is fine-tuned for life (consciousness). The reason is simply that the two have always eternally co-existed as two interrelated aspects of a single whole. With consciousness being necessary for matter to exist, and matter being necessary for consciousness to exist, and with each determining the attributes of the other. Thus, it is inevitable that the universe should have the life-giving parameters it does, and that life should emerge within it. As Thuan explains:

> According to Buddhism, consciousness has co-existed, co-exists and will co-exist with matter for all times. The same goes for the animate with the inanimate. Neither the universe nor consciousness had a beginning or end.

> Because they are interdependent, it is not surprising that the properties of the universe are compatible with the existence of consciousness. Two interdependent entities cannot exclude each other, but must be necessarily in harmony with each other. (2001: 213)

It should therefore hardly surprise us if the universe is in fact brimming with life. If Buddhism is correct, then this is exactly what we would expect the universe to be like.

As an aside, it is worth noting that, if the universe is brimming with life, theists could also use a similar strategy to argue for the existence of God. If it is absurdly improbable that the conditions necessary to sustain life should obtain purely by chance, and/or that life should emerge by chance even given those conditions, as explained earlier, then perhaps we are justified in seeking other explanations of these phenomena of which God may be the most reasonable. This is the gist of the so-called fine-tuning argument for the existence of God, according to which God is the best explanation of the apparent fine-tuning of the universe for life. Much more could be said, but there is insufficient space here to fully explore this argument so this brief summary will have to suffice. See Collins (2012) and Flew (2007) for a more detailed discussion of this argument.

Conclusion

Whilst our discussion of the major world religions has been all too brief, we can draw some conclusions from this (and the previous) section. We can see that none of the major world religions are threatened by the existence of ETIs. We can see that the Abrahamic faiths, because they are tied to certain historical events, places and people, do have to answer some, for want of a better word, 'awkward' questions – indeed, *problems* – for how intelligent aliens could fit into their theology. However, we've also seen that all three faiths possess the necessary intellectual resources to do this if necessary. Hinduism and Buddhism, especially, seem (wide) open to the possibility of alien life. Indeed, it almost seems like Hindus and Buddhists must endorse at least the possibility, and perhaps the actuality, of alien life. This raises an interesting possibility: what if we are *alone* in the universe? Does this pose a problem for Buddhism, Hinduism, or any other religion for that matter? This is something we will explore in the next section.

5 The Problem of God in a Lonely Universe

Most thinking around God and astrobiology concerns the implications that the existence (and/or discovery) of extraterrestrial life could, would, or should have for particular religious beliefs or believers. This is understandable, especially over a past century which saw giant leaps in space exploration, systematic scientific attempts to Search for Extraterrestrial Intelligence (SETI) in various ways (Shostak 2009; Cooper 2019), and the serious establishment of astrobiology as a field of study, all of which has helped fuel a good deal of popular and media interest in UFOs (Bader et al. 2017: 107–28; Halperin 2020), and countless successful films, TV series, and novels. Given all this, it would be strange if religious scholars, leaders, and no doubt countless lay adherents had not been prompted to ask themselves 'What if . . . ?'.

As we have seen, much of the existing philosophical and theological work in these areas has mostly explored whether, and if so how, specific religious traditions might be able to accommodate or incorporate extraterrestrial life, *should there turn out to be any*, within their doctrines and worldviews. That is to say, the focus has been on their 'openness', or not, to astrobiology. Incidentally, it is worth noting that empirical studies of what 'ordinary' religious people think about these topics generally find them to be relaxed at the prospect of 'contact'. A 2008 American survey, for example, found majorities from different religious traditions disagreeing with the statement that 'Official confirmation of the discovery of a civilization of intelligent beings living on another planet would so undercut the beliefs of my particular religious tradition that my religious tradition would face a crisis.' These included, *inter alia*, 67 per cent of Catholics, 73 per cent of Evangelical Protestants, 78 per cent of Jews, 95 per cent of Mormons, and 99 per cent of Buddhists (Peters 2009; Peters 2014: 265–7).

Note that *openness* to astrobiology is not the same thing as definitely *affirming* it. It is one thing to argue that, say, orthodox Muslim theology can quite happily accommodate the existence of ETIs – and if such were ever discovered, then no doubt various prooftexts would be brought forward as pointing to this fact all along. But it is quite another thing to say that orthodox Muslim theology is *committed* to there being intelligent life, or even life at all, elsewhere in the universe. No doubt there are some who would argue this. But many theologians who believe that (intelligent) astrobiology is perfectly *compatible* with Islamic doctrine, would probably remain agnostic as to whether there actually is any. And much the same would be true in other religious traditions. Classical Hindu and Buddhist cosmology is perfectly happy with the idea of there being all kinds of non-human intelligent beings, inhabiting all manner of different realms (Little 2021: 50–1). These *could* be taken to include other naturally evolved lifeforms on other planets within our physical universe. Indeed, as discussed in the previous section, this is arguably the most natural way of reading some of the texts in question. But other interpretations are, naturally, possible. (For example, perhaps these other universes are a metaphorical way of describing parallel dimensions or planes of existence, as with the 'Buddha fields' of Mahayana and Vajrayana Buddhism such as the Amitabha's 'Pure Land'.)

Suppose, however, that the Rare Earth hypothesis is true, and that on the scarce occasions that life does emerge in the universe, it is vanishingly unlikely ever to produce highly intelligent, morally self-aware creatures. Suppose also that, even if it did, the chances of these developing the type of socially complex, technologically advanced 'exocivilization' capable of interplanetary travel or communication is wildly remote (Cobb 2016; Sandberg et al. 2018). This Lonely Universe Hypothesis, while a minority view among contemporary astrobiology writers, is a scientifically credible one.

Even for religious traditions that do not explicitly affirm the existence of life elsewhere in the universe, a near-lifeless, barren universe might feasibly present some interesting problems of its own. (We leave aside the epistemological question of how this could ever be known. After all, there might always be life somewhere in the *next* galaxy on our to-explore list.) Why would an omnipotent, creative God make so vast a universe only to populate one infinitesimal corner of it? 'If it is just us, an awful lot of space is going to waste', as a character in the 1997 film version of Carl Sagan's *Contact* succinctly puts it (albeit not with reference to God). The issue here is not so much to do with *efficiency*, as though God has limited resources at his disposal. But rather a basic intuition that, given life's 'endless forms most wonderful and most beautiful' (Darwin 1859: 490) produced on Earth, it might perhaps be *fitting* for God to paint similarly on a much larger canvas. This 'principle of plenitude' (McMullin 2000: 163) was, for example, a large part of Thomas Paine's theological (or, given his Deist convictions, perhaps *deo*logical) argument in favour of there being life on other worlds:

> If we take a survey of our own world . . . we find every part of it, the earth, the waters, the air that surround it, filled, and as it were, crowded with life . . . Since then no part of our life is left unoccupied, why is it to be supposed, that the immensity of space is a naked void, lying in eternal waste . . .
>
> Our ideas, not only of the almightiness of the Creator, but of his wisdom and his beneficence, become enlarged in proportion as we contemplate the extent and structure of the universe. The solitary idea of a solitary world rolling, or at rest, in the immense ocean of space, gives place to the cheerful idea of a society of worlds . . . (1794: 41–6)

God(s) *as* Astrobiology

What, though, of religious traditions that are not merely open to astrobiology, but explicitly and categorically affirm it? Obviously, a lack of astrobiology would create serious problems to any group doctrinally committed to its existence. There are, as it happens, quite a lot of these.

The largest, and perhaps oldest, of them is the Church of Jesus Christ of Latter-day Saints, most commonly known as Mormonism, founded by Joseph Smith in the early nineteenth century. The Mormon scriptures speak plainly of there being 'worlds without number' (*Book of Moses*, 1.33), and that the 'inhabitants thereof are begotten sons and daughters unto God' (*Doctrines and Covenants*, 76.24). Smith's own preaching, moreover, was clear that 'God himself was once as we are now, and is an exalted man, and sits enthroned in yonder heavens!' (Smith [1844] 1971). On this view, God the Father, the Creator of our Earth, used to be 'a man like us' who 'dwelt on an earth' (ibid.) – presumably one of the other inhabited, extraterrestrial 'worlds' – in the remote past. If this interpretation is correct, then early Mormonism, at least, was committed to the existence of extraterrestrial 'humans' – indeed, 'if you were to see him today, you would see him like a man in form – like yourselves in all the person, image, and very form as a man' (Smith [1844] 1971) – of the kinds discussed in Section 3. Accordingly, other early Latter-day Saints leaders were perfectly comfortable with astrobiological speculation. Brigham Young, Smith's successor, even thought it likely that the Sun was inhabited (Weintraub 2014: 158). Strange as this idea might sound, it had been seriously mooted by the eminent astronomer William Herschel in the late eighteenth century: 'I think myself authorized, *upon astronomical principles*, to propose the sun as an inhabitable world'; 'it is most probably also inhabited, like the rest of the planets, by beings whose organs are adapted to the peculiar circumstances of that vast globe' (1795: 63; see Crowe 2001: 215–7).

Mormonism is but an early example of what would, in the twentieth century, develop into a steady stream of new religious movements with a significant astrobiological element. Some of the biggest and best-known examples include Scientology, founded in the 1950s by science fiction author L. Ron Hubbard, which includes an elaborate 'space opera' origins story (Rothstein 2009; Urban 2011: 73–82), and Raëlism, stemming from the 'contactee' experiences of Claude Vorilhon ('the prophet Raël'), which posits that humans were genetically engineered by a benevolent race of aliens known as the Elohim (Palmer 2004; Dericquebourg 2021). However, there are dozens of other examples (see Reese 2007; Zeller 2021).

'Where Is Their God?'

One feature held in common by several 'UFO religions' is a conviction that advanced beings have been or are communicating, often telepathically, with one or more favoured members of the group. Of course, communications from or with 'the other side' have been a frequent feature of many religious traditions, and can take many forms: dreams, visions, apparitions, the channelling of prophecies or oracles, creative or intellectual inspiration, mystical transports or journeys. Typically, however, these 'other sides' are understood as some metaphysical realm, outside of normal time and space. Advanced extraterrestrials, however, inhabit the same physical universe as we do. Accordingly, the ethereal 'other side' is transposed to the other side of the solar system or galaxy. Nevertheless, it is likewise often envisaged as being a place of quasi-heavenly peace and harmony. (Incidentally, in Liu Cixin's novel *The Three-Body Problem* there is an amusing situation following first contact between Earth and Trisolaris. The denizens of each, disillusioned with their own deeply imperfect worlds, start to venerate what they falsely imagine to be the perfections of their far-off counterparts ([2008] 2014).)

If, as is often the case, the supposed location of the communicating aliens is either unclear, or else is somewhere sufficiently far-off – bearing in mind that the closest solar system to our own, Alpha Centauri, is still four light-years away – then the claim is, in practice, comfortably unfalsifiable. However, some of the earliest twentieth-century UFO religions situated their extraterrestrial 'gods' squarely on one or more of our neighbouring planets. Venus was a popular choice, and featured heavily in both science fiction and UFO lore (e.g., George Adamski's two best-selling 'travelogues' 1953's *The Flying Saucers Have Landed* and 1955's *Inside the Space Ships*, following his alleged meeting with a Venusian named Orthon).

The Aetherius Society was founded in 1955, after a London taxi driver named George King purportedly began receiving messages from one Aetherius, a 'Cosmic Master' from Venus. In these and later messages, received over several decades, it emerged that other Venusian Cosmic Masters have included Jesus and the Buddha. Other planets, including Mars and Saturn, have their own, several of whom have appeared on Earth as great religious figures such as Krishna and Laozi. These highly evolved Masters have joined together, like a sort of celestial, interfaith Power Rangers, on a mission to save the cosmos – not least from humanity, as the mess they are making of their own planet risks spilling over into space. George King was thus chosen to help enlist a Fifth Column of earthlings, dreaming of a better world.

There is much more that could be said about the Aetherius Society. Our interest here lies in the fact that, since King first began channelling Aetherius, spacecraft have now visited Venus, Mars, and Saturn, and found neither Cosmic Masters nor life of any sort. Venus, in particular, is about as far from an Arcadia-like paradise as it is possible to be. Serious astronomy publications, not prone to hyperbole, often refer to it as 'a hellscape': a 900°F planet of volcanoes, swathed in clouds of sulfuric acid.

The empirical confirmation that ours is, if not necessarily a lonely universe, then at least a lonely solar system, looks as though it should pose a fatal problem for a religious system predicated on 'highly evolved, wise, beautiful and peace loving aliens from our neighbouring planets' (Rothstein 2021: 454). Indeed, the Aetherius Society at least acknowledges the *apparent* problem here. (In 2019, e.g., the New Zealand branch advertised an event on 'Spiritual Masters from Other Planets' with the questions: 'Jesus was from Venus? Buddha too? How can this be so if science tells us there is no intelligent life out there?'). In fact, the official solution to the problem is quite simple, and can be stated quite briefly:

> Civilizations, ancient beyond conception, exist on Mars, Venus, Saturn and other planets in the Solar System. So spiritually and technologically advanced are these civilizations that they vibrate at a higher frequency – on planes of existence as yet undetectable by terrestrial science. (Aetherius Society 2019)

This kind of saving qualification will be familiar to philosophers of religion (see Wisdom 1945; Flew [1950] 2000). It allows the true believers to protect a hitherto straightforward empirical claim from decisive falsification, while still maintaining that it is a factual assertion which could – and one day will be (*'as yet* undetectable', note) – proven.

'How Long, O Lord?'

An analogous type of problem, also resulting from an absence of predicted astrobiology, occurs in other groups whose 'gods' are alien superbeings. The last century has witnessed several examples of UFO religions that have pre-dicted the showily unambiguous advent of alien visitors – for example, as a 'We Come in Peace'-type Embassy to world leaders, or in the form of a mother ship descending to save an elect few (i.e., the group members) from an impending catastrophe – on or by a specific date (see Tumminia and Swatos 2001).

An early example was a small group known as 'the Seekers', who formed in Chicago in 1953. They centred around Dorothy Martin, a suburban housewife, who since the late 1940s had been receiving messages from a being known initially as Elder Brother, and later as Sananda, which is a common title in Theosophy (one of several influences Martin shared with both Adamski and King) for the spiritual Master, one of whose past lives had been the historical Jesus. Over time, Martin and other Seekers received multiple messages from various beings, known collectively as 'The Guardians', hailing from the planet Clarion and others. Most importantly, Martin channelled warnings that the mid-West would be the epicentre for a global cataclysm, engulfing America in earthquakes and tidal wives of such ferocity that the continent would be split in two. These upheavals would also raise the lost continents of Mu and Atlantis, and sink England, France and Russia to the bottom of the ocean. The date set for this apocalyptic chastisement was 21 December 1954. Fortunately for Martin and the others, she also received assurances that the righteous few 'will be gathered up and relieved of the experiences of the holocausts of the coming events' (quoted in Festinger et al. 1956: 48–59).

The group released this prophecy to the newspapers, which in turn attracted a team of social psychologists from the University Minnesota who then joined the group, under cover, to study what followed. Hence we have an invaluable, real-time account of the Seekers' individual and collective thoughts, feelings, and actions. (That said, the extent to which the researchers themselves, however inadvertently, affected the group dynamics itself complicates things. Not least, the sudden influx of these new, clearly well-educated, out-of-town 'converts' was received by the group as a *sign*: 'We had unintentionally reinforced their beliefs that Guardians were watching over humanity and were "sending" chosen people for special instruction about the cataclysm and the belief system' (240).)

A few days before the appointed time, Martin received a phone call from a 'Captain Video' informing her that a flying saucer would come by the house to collect them at 4pm on 20 December. Suggestions that this might be a hoax were quickly quelled. The group gathered early that afternoon, having dutifully removed all metal from their persons, in accordance with earlier travel advice from the Guardians. 4pm, however, came and went. More messages, apologizing for the delay, were received; a new time of 11.30pm was given. This too passed. Ultimately, at the end of a sleepless night spent agonizing over possible explanations for the let-down – at one point a message came from Clarion, helpfully suggesting they break for coffee – Martin received a new revelation: 'Not since the beginning of time upon this Earth has there been such a force of Good and light as now floods this room and that which has been loosed within this room now floods the entire Earth' (171). In short, thanks to the faith and virtue of the Seekers, the coming cataclysm had been averted. And since there was no disaster, no flying saucer was now needed to come and rescue them.

Other UFO groups have dealt with failed prophecies in a roughly analogous fashion. The Unarius Academy of Science, also founded in the mid-1950s, had long expected an armada of 'Space Brothers' to arrive in 2001 (a year with a suitable space-y gravitas, thanks to Stanley Kubrick and Arthur C. Clarke); itself a postponement from the originally prophesied 1976. When 2001 came and went, however, 9/11 and its aftermath was revealed as having caused an indefinite delay: 'war kept the Space Brothers away. [The Unarians] did not find fault with their teachings, but with the negative energies that humans continued to create from their lower selves' (Tumminia 2005: 95–8). Note that, while it was the Seekers' merit that vicariously saved humanity from deserved destruction, here it is humanity's unrepentant iniquity that denies us the joyous day of 'first contact' with the Interplanetary Federation. (Perhaps not surprisingly, Unarians feel a great affinity with *Star Trek*, to the point of some watching old episodes to help remind them of their past lives.)

Not all such groups end up solving the problem in this semi-standard way, however. Most notably, Heaven's Gate was a small, close-knit UFO group, started in Texas in the mid-1970s. It combined Christian apocalypticism, New Age ideas, and sci-fi themes, and members severed themselves from their families and friends to live a communal life of radical asceticism; some members went so far as to castrate themselves in pursuit of sexual purity. The founders, Marshall Applewhite and Bonnie Nettles, saw themselves as envoys from a race of immortal aliens, whose present mission was to usher in the Apocalypse as the 'two witnesses' of Revelation 11. Salvation, on this schema, involves a process of spiritual and physical transformation to 'The Evolutionary Level Above Human': 'adherents believed that they would physically transform their bodies into perfected extraterrestrial creatures and physically journey to the Next Level aboard a UFO' (Zeller 2014: 165). It was this Level from which Jesus Christ – as, according to the group's theology, Applewhite had been known on a prior earthly sojourn – descended during his Incarnation, and to which he returned at his Ascension (with 'the cloud' of Acts 1.9 being naturally interpreted as a UFO).

Similar to the Seekers, Heaven's Gate members expected that a UFO would descend to save the faithful few from the tribulations engulfing the rest of Earth's *massa damnata*. However, Nettles died from cancer in 1985, awkwardly before 'the Two' had yet triggered the End Times. A decade later, the group's numbers were down to a few dozen, and new converts had mostly dried up – despite attempts to interest *Star Trek* fans with messages from 'The Real Q' (a powerful, godlike alien who appears across the *Next Generation*, *Deep Space 9*, and *Voyager* series; see Peterson 1999) on internet message boards. Still no UFO came to carry them off to – or in Applewhite's case, back to – the Next Level.

Rather than wait for a UFO physically to come to them, the idea formed that they might need to go to *it*. But to do that, they would first need to shed their earthly bodies. Scholars debate precisely how and why the community came to take the final, radical step. Certainly, they retained a belief in the Apocalypse being imminent: 'This planet is about to be recycled, refurbished, started over' (quoted in Zeller 2014: 199). It seems they were waiting for a sign revealing their cue to leave.

For a group so primed, the spectacular appearance in the night skies of a hitherto unknown comet, Hale-Bopp, could hardly have seemed a coincidence. First spotted in May 1995, Hale-Bopp was visible to the naked eye throughout 1996 and well into 1997. Wild rumours circulated online and on late-night radio about an alleged second object, thought by some to be a spacecraft, flying along in its wake. The comet passed closest to Earth on 22 March 1997. That very day, Applewhite and thirty-eight followers, dressed identically in *Star Trek*-style costumes with self-designed 'Away Team' badges, began a carefully orchestrated mass suicide. Among the group's last acts, they mailed out a press release entitled 'Heaven's Gate "Away Team" Returns to Level Above Human in Distant Space' along with videotaped farewell messages. At least four others, three (former) members and another with no previous connection to the group, took what Heaven's Gate materials termed the 'Last Chance to Leave' in the following months.

Conclusion

Most current work in astrotheology or exophilosophy proceeds on the assumption, howsoever hypothetically held, that there are or might be alien life-forms *out there*. Accordingly, most of our attention in this Element has focused on the various theological and philosophical problems arising from such possibilities.

In this section, conversely, we have considered the problems arising for different religious belief systems from there being either no astrobiology, or at least no astrobiology in the right (i.e., predicted, prophesied) places and times. We have briefly looked at several case-studies: Paine's Deism, Mormonism, the Aetherius Society, the Seekers, the Unarius Academy of Science, and Heaven's Gate. Evidently, the problems of God and astrobiology are not always purely abstract ones.

In the next section, we turn to our final frontier of astrotheological speculation, albeit one implicit in much of this section too. In short, what if astrobiology doesn't create problems for God-beliefs, but is instead the *solution* to the age-old 'problem of God' itself?

6 Atheism and (Ancient) Astrobiology

As we have seen, there are quite a number of religious groups, mostly founded in the past century, whose 'gods' are, in fact, very advanced extraterrestrial beings. So far in advance of us, in fact – 'The Evolutionary Level Above Human' for Heaven's Gate; 'on planes of existence as yet undetectable by terrestrial science' for the Aetherius Society – that they are sufficiently spiritually, morally, and technologically gifted as to fulfil the role that at least the gods (if not the God of Classical Theism) have traditionally held in the human imagination. Alternatively, worth noting here too is the suggestion that, in an increasingly secular world, beliefs in UFOs or alien abductions may function as substitutes for more traditionally religious beliefs (Pasulka 2019; Halperin 2020).

Here, however, we will consider some more obviously secular attempts at providing *extraterrestrial explanations* for reports about God/s and his/their interactions with humanity, as well as of certain features of the world sometimes thought as offering evidence for divine intervention. Proponents of such ideas often refer to them under the umbrella term of the 'Ancient Astronaut Hypothesis' (AAH).

Ancient Astronaut Hypothesis (AAH)

In its most basic form, the AAH proposes that where, for example, the great scriptures of the world's religions relate stories about God or gods, or miracles wrought by them, or of human beings talking to or inspired by them, these are most plausibly and rationally interpreted as reports of advanced extraterrestrial beings ('ancient astronauts') and the various ways in which they have interacted with humanity throughout our history. Of course, so the argument goes, pre-scientific and pre-technological human beings had no way of conceiving of, or speaking about, visitors from other planets with highly sophisticated technologies other than in the mythological, metaphorical language of supernatural beings with miraculous powers.

> Whatever was described in the Old Testament wasn't 'God'. It was a misunderstood flesh-and-blood extraterrestrial whom our ancestors misunderstood as being divine and supernatural. Why? Because of misunderstood technology. And that is the underlying thread that applies to all of the Ancient Astronaut theory. (Giorgio Tsoukalos, in Ancient Aliens 2010a)

> In the Ancient Astronaut opinion, the whole pantheon of gods that we have in ancient Greece consists of nothing else but flesh-and-blood extraterrestrials who were misinterpreted as being these divine creatures by our ancestors. (Giorgio Tsoukalos, in Ancient Aliens 2010b)

To be sure, some scriptural texts are especially amenable to this kind of hermeneutical approach. Thus the Jewish and Christian scriptures' 'chariots of fire and horses of fire' by which 'Elijah ascended into heaven by a whirlwind' (2 Kings 2.11), and the curious 'wheels within wheels' of Ezkeiel's angelic visitors (Ezekiel 1), are taken as fairly clear attempts at describing spacecraft: 'Wheels and chariots were as close as biblical people came to anything we would call technology. Computers and lasers were not in their lexicon' (Downing [1968] 2019: loc. 351). Similar interpretive claims have been made about the flying chariots, or *vimāna*s, which appear in the Vedic literature of early Hinduism (see Little 2021), or indeed for the 'horse' named Buraq ('Lightning') conveying Muhammad on his 'night journey' from Mecca to Jerusalem and heaven, according to Islamic hadith traditions (Ancient Aliens 2013).

Flashing, flying 'machines', transporting either humans to the heavens, or else celestial beings to Earth, are purely the most obvious, entry-level examples of AAH explanations. Other scriptural episodes require much greater elaboration, and admit of a wi(l)der range of possibilities. For instance, might the Israelites' Ark of the Covenant have been a portable nuclear reactor, powering a machine for manufacturing edible algae (i.e., 'manna'), which one day a week (i.e., the Sabbath) needed to be shut down for cleaning and maintenance work (Ancient Aliens 2010a, 2019)? Or was it instead an electric radio set permitting Moses to communicate with the powerful alien (i.e., 'the Lord') inside the spaceship (i.e., 'the pillar of the fire') shepherding the Hebrew people through the desert (von Däniken [1968] 2019: 50)? Alternatively, it could have been a high-tech weapon of some kind: 'Was the Ark of the Covenant a modified Tesla coil that spewed out deadly fireballs in every direction around the device? It is an interesting thought and it would explain why falling face-first onto the ground, as Moses and Aaron did, could save a person's life, as the fireballs would be flying over their heads' (Childress 2016: 77).

A great many more examples could be given. Indeed, the AAH's most successful proponents, Swiss author Erich von Däniken (1935–) and the History Channel's documentary series *Ancient Aliens* (2009–), have so far filled over forty books and 230 episodes respectively with this kind of theorizing, drawing on myriad religious and mythological sources. These are not, however, the only types of evidence that AAH theorists bring forward to support their case. Ancient art supposedly depicting astronauts or ahead-of-the-time technologies are often appealed to. So too are various examples of pre-modern architecture and engineering – the Pyramids, for example – which, it is argued, would have been completely beyond the capacities of the people whom traditional archaeology claims created them. To quote Giorgio Tsoukalos, a mentee of von Däniken's and the main star of *Ancient Aliens*:

> It defies logic that our early ancestors, with their limited technology, could have built these gigantic megalithic structures with the most gigantic stones all on their own. I think that all those ancient monuments ... were built with sophisticated technology and under the tutelage of extraterrestrials. (2016: 84)

More fundamentally, some AAH theorists point to the overall capacities of human beings as a species, and how swiftly civilization has developed over the past several thousand years from hunter-gatherers to planetary explorers, as pointing to some manner of deliberate stewardship on the part of superior beings. Different versions of this basic idea – which, we may note, has clear parallels with some Creationist and/or Intelligent Design theorizing – include one or more of selective breeding, human-alien hybridization, or (in its more recent iterations) genetic engineering (e.g., Sitchin 1976; von Däniken 2017).

AAH as a 'Fringe Science'

As is clear from the above, AAH theorists draw on a wide range of sources and types of evidence. In the space of a single episode, for example, *Ancient Aliens* might draw on texts from a half-dozen religions, mythological stories from Greece and Scandinavia, and archaeological sites in Mesopotamia and Latin America, with commentary from a range of convinced AAH theorists and/or fellow travellers from the 'alternative archaeology' (Moshenska 2017) milieu. The absence of any AAH-critical views is an intentional design choice. According to the show's creator and Executive Producer: 'We ... made a deliberate decision to not populate the program with the usual phalanx of naysayers, skeptics, and debunkers. Not because we didn't want balance, mind you. It was simply because we wanted our show to be open-minded' (Burns 2016: ix).

The eclectic, even scattergun, nature of the evidence presented makes it hard to critique *in toto*. There is no discrete set of facts or arguments upon which the AAH stands or falls. Von Däniken himself admits that some of the examples in his millions-selling 1968 book *Chariots of the Gods?*, which although not the first in this genre was and remains very much the landmark text, are 'Total poppycock!' ([1999] 2019). Furthermore, the rhetorical strategy of AAH theorists is frequently that of the 'only asking questions' variety:

> Despite some of the erroneous data, no corner pillar of my 'think tank' has been brought to collapse. And here's what the critics overlooked: In *Chariots of the Gods*, there are 323 question marks. Questions are the opposite of assertions. (von Däniken 2019)

Despite all this, it is important to note that across all the various fields touched upon – history, archaeology, linguistics, biblical studies, etc. – a great many specific claims made by AAH theorists have been decisively debunked (e.g., Story 1976; Fagan 2006; Colavito 2020). Most professional scholars who have commented on the AAH, or at least on those aspects of it which touch on their particular areas of expertise, would thus likely agree with the assessment of Isaac Asimov:

> While there is nothing inconceivable about visits to Earth by extraterrestrial civilizations in the past, even in the near past, there is no acceptable evidence that it has happened, and the evidence deduced for the purpose by various enthusiasts is, as far as we can tell, utterly worthless. (1981: 223)

Accordingly, it would be fair to categorize AAH as a classic example of 'pseudoscience', or perhaps more neutrally, 'fringe science' (Gordin 2021: 54–5). In common with other fringe sciences – cryptozoology, astrology – whose subject areas overlap with, but are fundamentally at odds with, established domains of academic enquiry, many AAH theorists see this 'outsider', 'maverick' position as a source of pride (Gordin 2021: 41–3).

Atheism and the AAH

The AAH is, much to the chagrin of many professional archaeologists, undoubtedly popular. Von Däniken is by no means the only multimillion-selling author in this world. *Ancient Aliens* is one of America's (and indeed, the globe's) most popular documentary series, and has spawned books, an eponymous computer game, and regular 'AlienCon' conventions attended by tens of thousands. Also noteworthy here is the extent to which AAH-inspired ideas are present within popular culture. Classic science fiction, including H. P. Lovecraft's 'The Call of Cthulu' (1928), Arthur C. Clarke's *Childhood's End* (1953) and *2001: A Space Odyssey* (1968; Stanley Kubrick's celebrated film version came out the same year), and Frank Herbert's *The Godmakers* (1972), has played with the basic idea. So too have big-budget Hollywood movies including *Stargate* (1994), *The X-Files: Fight the Future* (1998), and *Indiana Jones and the Kingdom of the Crystal Skull* (2008). Among several examples from television, perhaps the most entertaining is in the original *Star Trek* series, where the Enterprise happens upon the planet to which the Greek 'god' – in fact, a megalomaniacal alien – Apollo is spending his post-Earth retirement (1968's 'Who Mourns for Adonais?'; see Asa 1999).

For these reasons, the significance of the AAH as a carrier and propagator of atheistic and/or agnostic ideas should not be overlooked. This may well be a very different variety of unbelieving to the kind that most readily springs to many people's minds: that associated with philosophers such as Bertrand Russell and A. C. Grayling, or unimpeachably *non*-fringe scientists like Richard Dawkins and Neil DeGrasse Tyson, for example. Nevertheless, a large proportion of AAH theory consists of taking religious or mythological texts which explicitly refer to a God or gods, and offering a wholly naturalistic, materialist hypothesis, involving astrobiological beings (i.e., Tsoukalos' 'flesh-and-blood extraterrestrials') and advanced technology, in order to explain them. AAH explanations might seem weird or wild; one might even class them as 'paranormal' (cf. Bader et al. 2017). But note that they are not *supernatural* ones. Certainly, there *are* ufologists who propose strictly supernatural accounts of alleged extraterrestrial phenomena (there are, e.g., both Christians and

Muslims who ascribe UFOs to demonic forces). But such views are barely if ever referenced within typical AAH discourse where, indeed, the opposite is true. All manner of alleged supernatural beings, including angels, demons, fairies, and ghosts, are subjected to the standard explanation: 'Aliens!'

Conversely, theistic or otherwise supernatural explanations are normally presented as being, *ipso facto*, false. Hence, their assumed, inherent implausibility lends support for the *only other* possibility:

> There's only two possibilities – either God did it, which we really don't think happened, or some hi-tech civilization from another planet came ... (Giorgio Tsoukalos, in Ancient Aliens 2010)

> We have these stories of these 'gods' that have these supernatural, magical powers. Let's be honest, magical, supernatural powers don't really exist. So what was it that was described? In my opinion, it was people who had access to advanced technology. (Giorgio Tsoukalos, in Ancient Aliens 2014)

Of course, one might well point out that these are false dichotomies. Even if one is sceptical of a straightforwardly theistic/supernatural explanation of the text or alleged phenomenon in question, there could well be other reasonable explanations. For instance, if it is a textual source, perhaps the alleged miracle or divine appearance simply didn't happen as reported. Perhaps witnesses were fooled or confused, or the text was written many centuries after the events in question. Or perhaps the author is using poetic or metaphorical language. If it is a megalith or precision-engineered artefact, perhaps ancient peoples were capable of much more than the armchair archaeologist, otherwise almost wholly ignorant of the cultures in question, would guess. (After all, human beings built the Parthenon and Pantheon, the great medieval cathedrals, and the Taj Mahal, all without power tools or Computer Aided Design: not even AAH theorists claim that *these* required extraterrestrial assistance.)

However, by confining the choice to 'gods *versus* aliens', and simply assuming that it *can't* have been gods, then the way is cleared for aliens to win by default. One is reminded here of the famous dictum of Sherlock Holmes, that 'When you have eliminated the impossible, whatever remains, *however improbable*, must be the truth' (Conan Doyle 1890: 93). For the presumed audience of *Ancient Aliens*, what is 'impossible' is any reasonable theistic interpretation of the data.

The AAH functions, therefore, as a curious kind of *euhemerism*. Euhemerus of Messene was a fourth/third century BC Greek author. In his *Sacred History* (mostly lost, though parts are preserved by other writers), Euhemerus suggested that the classical gods were, way back in the remote past, originally a royal dynasty of Crete ('Uranus was the first king, a gentle and benevolent man . . .'). Over time, their various military and romantic exploits grew in the telling. It is no coincidence that Euhemerus was writing in the generation after Alexander the Great's remarkable life, at a time when he was already being worshipped as a god in many places, and when legends about him were increasing in both number and imagination (Brown 1946). Euhemerist interpretations are, therefore, attempts at offering alternative, naturalistic explanations for beliefs about God(s). This is, as we have seen, precisely what the AAH does.

That is not to say, however, that AAH proponents themselves are necessarily atheists. Indeed, several of the leading figures, including von Däniken and Tsoukalos, have explicitly denied this. For them, AAH explanations are perfectly compatible with belief in a higher, purer 'Something', which would presumably account for the existence of both us and the flesh-and-blood extraterrestrial 'gods'. After all, to explain human origins with reference to biological entities from other planets, raises the prior question as to *what* or *who* explains their origins. Likewise, if one situates the 'gods' *within* the cosmos, then one is still stuck with explaining the cosmos itself.

In practice, however, the great bulk of AAH theorizing functions in a straightforwardly atheistic manner, with any and all of the God(s) envisaged in the world's religious traditions seemingly 'fair game' for the Ancient Astronaut treatment. One could watch an awful lot of *Ancient Aliens* episodes, and never encounter the idea of there perhaps being a higher, purer God 'behind' all these demythologized accounts of extraterrestrial gods-falsely-so-called.

Final Thoughts on the Final Frontier

As noted at the beginning of this Element, the topic of 'God and astrobiology' is a wide-ranging one, encompassing exciting new research in astronomy, biology, and chemistry; the works of great philosophers, theologians, and novelists; popular movies and television shows; millennia-old religious traditions with millions of adherents and tiny 'cults' formed within living memory. Along the way, we have seen how 'astrobiology', in the broad sense of the term, poses all manner of interesting problems for beliefs about God (and/or gods), and has done for many centuries. In this final section, we have explored what is arguably the converse view: that is, that astrobiology is itself the ultimate answer to the where, how, and why human beings acquired many of those beliefs in the first place.

What conclusions can we draw from this whirlwind overview of astrobiology and exotheology? Well, in Section 2, we saw that the current goals and ambitions of astrobiology as a discipline are far more modest than many might imagine. Whilst organizations like SETI continue to search for intelligent extraterrestrial civilizations, the work of most astrobiologists is far more mundane, less a search for hyperintelligent, spacefaring Arcadians and more a search for single-celled, rock-dwelling Archaea. In Sections 3 and 4, we saw how all the major world religions can accommodate the existence and/or discovery of intelligent extraterrestrials, and we saw that the Vedic religions (Hinduism and Buddhism) are particularly receptive to the existence of such beings. In Section 5, we examined the opposite possibility: what if we are alone in the universe? We saw that whilst many of the major world religions are quite comfortable with this notion, certain new religious movements would struggle to accommodate such a possibility, although we also saw the different strategies these groups have used in the face of failed expectations of alien visitation. Finally, in Section 6, we saw that for some thinkers of an atheistic bent ETIs can, in certain respects, take the place of traditional conceptions of God/s, as per the AAH.

Whilst we may find life out there one day, and perhaps of an intelligent kind, at least for now the universe appears largely empty. Thus, much of the theorizing explored in this book is akin to the theorizing done to answer the medieval question, referenced in Section 1, '*Quid mus sumit?*' (Perhaps we should ask: '*Quid Homo extraterrestrialis sumit?*' Hopefully not us!) We explore these questions, then, not because we immediately need an answer or to fulfil a practical need. Nor do we even anticipate a final definitive answer to them. Rather, we explore these questions in order to clarify our theological and philosophical thinking which, in turn, are both ultimately attempts to understand *ourselves* and *our* place in the universe, whether or not we are alone.

References

Aetherius Society (2019). Spiritual Aliens – Why Are They Here? www
.aetherius.org/event/spiritual-aliens-why-are-they-here/.

Al-Khalili, Jim (2010). *Pathfinders: The Golden Age of Arabic Science*,
London: Allen Lane.

Ancient Aliens (2010a). The Evidence (History Channel). Season 1, episode 1,
first broadcast: 20 April 2010.

Ancient Aliens (2010b). The Visitors (History Channel). Season 1, episode 2,
first broadcast: 27 April 2010.

Ancient Aliens (2013). Strange Abductions (History Channel). Season 5, episode
9, first broadcast: 22 February 2013.

Ancient Aliens (2014). Aliens and Superheroes (History Channel). Season 8,
episode 9, first broadcast: 22 August 2014.

Ancient Aliens (2019). Food of the Gods (History Channel). Season 14, episode
18, first broadcast: 1 November 2019.

Aquinas, Thomas (1948). *Summa Theologica translated by the Fathers of the
English Dominican Province*, New York: Benziger Bros

Asa, Robert (1999). Classic *Star Trek* and the Death of God: A Case Study of
'Who Mourns for Adonais?'. In Jennifer E. Porter and Darcee L. McLaren,
eds., Star Trek *and Sacred Ground: Explorations of* Star Trek, *Religion, and
American Culture*, Albany, NY: State University of New York Press, 33–59.

Asimov, Isaac (1981). *Extraterrestrial Civilizations*, London: Pan.

Augustine (2012). *The City of God*, translated by William Babcock with notes
by Boniface Ramsey, Hyde Park: New City Press.

Bader, Christopher D., Joseph O. Baker, and F. Carson Mencken (2017).
*Paranormal America: Ghost Encounters, UFO Sightings, Bigfoot Hunts,
and Other Curiosities in Religion and Culture*, 2nd ed., New York:
New York University Press.

Baggini, Julian (2005). *The Pig That Wants to Be Eaten and Ninety-Nine Other
Thought Experiments*, London: Granta.

The Bhagavad Gita (2008). Translated by W. J. Johnson, Oxford University
Press: Oxford.

The Bhagavata Purana (2019) Translated by Bibek Debroy in three volumes,
Penguin Random House India: Delhi.

The Blob (1958). Directed by Irvin S. Yeaworth Jr. and Russell S. Doughten Jr.,
Hollywood, CA: Fairview Productions.

Bradbury, Ray (2008). *The Martian Chronicles*. London: Harper Collins

Brake, Mark (2013). *Alien Life Imagined: Communicating the Science and Culture of Astrobiology*, Cambridge: Cambridge University Press.

Briot, Danielle (2012). 'A Possible First Use of the Word Astrobiology?'. *Astrobiology* 12, no. 12, 1154–6. http://doi.org/10.1089/ast.2012.0896.

Brown, Truesdell S. (1946). Euhemerus and the Historians. *Harvard Theological Review* 39, no. 4, 259–74.

Bruce, Scott G. (2006). Hagiography as Monstrous Ethnography: A Note on Ratramnus of Corbie's Letter Concerning the Conversion of the Cynocephali. In Wieland, Gernot, Ruff, Carin, and Arthur, Ross G. eds., *Insignis Sophiae Arcator: Medieval Latin Studies in Honour of Michael Herren on his 65th Birthday*, Turnhout: Brepols Publishers.

Bullivant, Stephen (2011). *Sine culpa?* Vatican II and Inculpable Ignorance. *Theological Studies* 72, 70–86.

Burke-Gaffney, Michael W. (1937). Kepler and the Star of Bethlehem. *Journal of the Royal Astronomical Society of Canada* 31, 417–25.

Burl, Aubrey (1983). *Prehistoric Astronomy and Ritual*, London: Shire Books.

Burns, Kevin (2016). Foreword. In The Producers of Ancient Aliens, ed., *Ancient Aliens: The Official Companion Book*, San Francisco, CA: HarperOne, iii–xi.

Cai, X., Jiang, J. H., Fahy, K. A., and Yung, Y. L. (2021). A Statistical Estimation of the Occurrence of Extraterrestrial Intelligence in the Milky Way Galaxy. *Galaxies* 9, no. 5, 1–14. https://doi.org/10.3390/galaxies9010005.

Card, Orson Scott (1985). *Ender's Game*, New York: Tom Doherty Associates.

Card, Orson Scott (1986). *Speaker for the Dead*, New York: Tom Doherty Associates.

Catholic Church (1997). *Catechism of the Catholic Church*, Second Edition, Libreria Editrice Vaticana. www.usccb.org/sites/default/files/flipbooks/catechism/VI/ [accessed 24 March 2023]

Chapman, Allan (2002). *Gods in the Sky: Astronomy from the Ancients to the Renaissance*, London: Channel 4 Books.

Childress, David Hatcher (2016). *Ark Of God: The Incredible Power of the Ark of the Covenant*, Kempton, IL: Unlimited Adventures Press.

Clarke, Arthur C. (1953). *Childhood's End*, New York: Ballantine Books.

Clarke, Arthur C. (1955). The Star. https://sites.uni.edu/morgans/astro/course/TheStar.pdf [accessed 16 December 2022].

Clarke, Arthur C. (1968). *2001: A Space Odyssey*, London: Hutchinson.

Cleary, Thomas (1993). *The Flower Ornament Scripture: A Translation of the Avatamsaka Sutra*, Shambhala: London.

Cobb, Matthew (2016). Alone in the Universe: The Improbability of Alien Civilizations. In Jim Al-Khalili, ed., *Aliens: Science Asks: Is There Anyone Out There?* London: Profile, chap. 14

Colavito, Jason (2020). *The Mound Builder Myth: Fake History and the Hunt for a 'Lost White Race'*, Norman, OK: University of Oklahoma Press.

Collins, Robin (2012). The Teleological Argument: An Exploration of the Fine-Tuning of the Universe. In William Lane Craig and J. P. Moreland, eds., *The Blackwell Companion to Natural Theology*, Hoboken: Wiley-Blackwell, 202–81.

Conan Doyle, Arthur (1890). *The Sign of Four*, London: Spencer Blackett.

Connes, Pierre (2020). *History of the Plurality of Worlds: The Myths of Extraterrestrials Through the Ages*, J. Lequeux, ed., New York: Springer Cham.

Cooper, Keith (2019). *The Contact Paradox: Challenging Our Assumptions in the Search for Extraterrestrial Intelligence*, London: Bloomsbury.

Craig, William Lane and Moreland, Jame Porter (2012). *The Blackwell Companion to Natural Theology*, Hoboken: Wiley-Blackwell.

Crowe, Michael J. (1997). A History of the Extraterrestrial Life Debate. *Zygon* 32, no. 2, 147–62. https://doi.org/10.1111/0591-2385.801997079.

Crowe, Michael J. (2001). Astronomy and Religion (1780-1915): Four Case Studies Involving Ideas of Extraterrestrial Life. *Osiris* 16, 209–26.

Darwin, Charles (1859). *On the Origin of Species by Means of Natural Selection, or the Preservation of Favoured Races in the Struggle for Life*, London: John Murray.

Dericquebourg, Régis (2021). Rael and the Raleians. In Benjamin E. Zeller, ed., *Handbook of UFO Religions*, Leiden: Brill, 472–90.

Desai, J. G. (2003). The Hindu View of the Natural World. *Nidan* 15, 57–68.

Determann, Jörg Matthias (2020). *Islam, Science Fiction and Extraterrestrial Life: The Culture of Astrobiology in the Muslim World*. New York: Bloomsbury.

Dick, Steven J. (1982). *Plurality of Worlds: The Origins of the Extraterrestrial Life Debate from Democritus to Kant*, Cambridge: Cambridge University Press.

Downing, Barry ([1968] 2019). *The Bible and Flying Saucers: Did a UFO Part the Red Sea?* Independently Published.

Dutton, Paul Edward (2004). *Carolingian Civilization: A Reader*, 2nd ed., Peterborough: Broadview Press.

Elzembely, Hosam A. Ibrahim, and Emad El-Din Aysha (eds.) (2021). *Arab and Muslim Science Fiction: Critical Essays*, Jefferson, NC: McFarland.

Ekstrom, Laura W. (2023). *Evil and Theodicy*, Cambridge: Cambridge University Press.

Fagan, Garrett G. (2006). *Archaeological Fantasies: How Pseudoarchaeology Misrepresents the Past and Misleads the Public*, London: Routledge.

Festinger, Leon, Henry Riecken, and Stanley Schachter (1956). *When Prophecy Fails: A Social and Psychological Study of a Modern Group that Predicted the Destruction of the World*, New York: Harper-Torchbooks.

Flew, Antony ([1950] 2000). Theology and Falsification: A Golden Jubilee Celebration. *Philosophy Now* 29, 28–9

Flew, Anthony (2007). *There is a God: How the World's Most Notorious Atheist Changed His Mind*, New York: HarperCollins.

Foltz, Bruce (2019). *Medieval Philosophy: A Multicultural Reader*, London: Bloomsbury.

Fontenelle, Bernard Le Bovier de ([1686] 1803). *Conversations on the Plurality of Worlds*, E. Gunning, trans., London: T. Hurst.

Śrī Garga-saṃhitā (2006). Translated by Danavir Goswami and Kuśakratha Dāsa Rupanuga, Kansas City, MO: Vedic College.

Gordin, Michael D. (2021). *On the Fringe: Where Science Meets Pseduoscience*, New York: Oxford University Press.

Hahn, Scott (2007). *Reasons to Believe*. New York: Doubleday

Haider, Shahbaz, Abdullah Ansar, and Syed Ali Asdaq Naqvi (2023). Shīʿī Imāmī Thought on Existence, Life, and Extraterrestrials. *Theology and Science* 21, no. 2, 261–72.

Halperin, David J. (2020). *Intimate Alien: The Hidden Story of the UFO*, Stanford, CA: Stanford University Press.

Herbert, Frank (1972). *The Godmakers*, New York: Putnam.

Herodian. ([c. 245] 1961). *History of the Roman Empire*, trans. Edward C. Echols, Berkeley, CA: University of California Press.

Herschel, William (1795). On the Nature and Construction of the Sun and Fixed Stars. *Philosophical Transactions of the Royal Society of London* 85, 46-72.

Ibn 'Arabi Muhyi-al-din (1972). *al-Futahat al-makkiyyah*, edited by Osman Yahya in 14 vols. Beirut: Dar Sader.

Ioannides, Mara Wendy Cohen (2019). 'Judaism and Extraterrestrials: Theological Lessons from Science Fiction' *The Journal of Popular Culture* 52, no. 5, 1200–17.

Iqbal, Muzaffar (2018). Islamic Theology Meets ETI. In Ted Peters, Martinez Hewlett, Joshua M. Moritz, and Robert John Russell, eds., *Astrotheology: Science and Theology Meet Extraterrestrial Life*, Oregon: Cascade Books, 216–27.

Kaufman, Marc (n.d.). *Life, Here and Beyond*, https://astrobiology.nasa.gov/about/ [Accessed 11 May 2023].

al-Kis'I, Muhammad ibn 'Ali (1978). *The Tales of the Prophets*, translated with notes by W. M. Thackston Jr., Boston: Twayne Publishers.

Krishnamurthy, Visvanatha (2019). *Meet the Ancient Scriptures of Hinduism*, Chennai: Notion Press.

Lamm, Norman (1965). The Religious Implications of Extraterrestrial Life. *Tradition: A Journal of Orthodox Jewish Thought* 7, no. 8, 5–56.

Lewis, C. S. (1938). *Out of the Silent Planet*, London: John Lane.

Lewis, C. S. (1943). *Perelandra*, London: Bodley Head.

Lewis, C. S. (1945). *That Hideous Strength: A Modern Fairy-Tale for Grown-Ups*, London: Bodley Head.

Little, Layne R. (2021). Vimānas and Hindu Ufology. In Benjamin E. Zeller, ed., *Handbook of UFO Religions*, Leiden: Brill, 39–78.

Liu, Cixin ([2008] 2014). *The Three-Body Problem*, trans. Ken Liu, London: Head of Zeus.

Loike, John D., and Tendler, Moshe D. (2003). Ma Adam Va-teda-ehu: Halakhic Criteria for Defining Human Beings. *Tradition: A Journal of Orthodox Jewish Thought* 37, no. 2, 1–19.

Losch, Andreas and Krebs, Andreas (2015). Implications for the Discovery of Extraterrestrial Life: A Theological Approach. *Theology and Science* 13, no. 2, 230–44, https://doi.org/10.1080/14746700.2015.1023522.

Lovecraft, H. P. (1928). The Call of Cthulu. www.hplovecraft.com/writings/texts/fiction/cc.aspx [accessed 25 April 2023].

Macy, Gary (1991). Of Mice and Manna: *Quid Mus Sumit* as a Pastoral Question. *Recherches de théologie ancienne et médiévale* 58, 157–166.

Mahabharata (1883-1896). Translated by Kisari Mohan Ganguli. www.sacred-texts.com/hin/maha/ [Accessed 26 April 2023].

Malik, Shoaib Ahmed and Determann, Jörg Matthias (eds.) (2024). *Islamic Theology and Extraterrestrial Life: New Frontiers in Science and Religion*, London: I.B. Tauris. www.bloomsbury.com/uk/islamic-theology-and-extraterrestrial-life-9780755650880/#:~:text=This%20book%20explains%20how%20such,contrast%20Islamic%20perspectives%20with%20Christianity.

Manuaba, I. B. Arya Lawa and Sudirman, I. Nyoman (2018) 'Descriptions of Aliens (Extraterrestrial Beings) in Vedic Scriptures', *Vidyottama Sanatana* 2, no. 2, 203–10.

Masood, Ehsan (2009). *Islam and Science: A History*, London: Icon Books.

Matter, Ann E. (2006). The Soul of the Dog-Man: Ratramnus of Corbie Between Theology and Philosophy. *Rivista di Storia della Filosofia* 61, no. 1, Filosofie e Teologie, 43–53.

McColley, Grant and Miller, H. W. (1937). Saint Bonaventure, Francis Mayron, William Vorilong, and the Doctrine of a Plurality of Worlds. *Speculum* 12, no. 3, 386–9.

McIntosh, Chad A. and McNabb, Tyler Dalton (2021). Houston, Do We Have a Problem? Extraterrestrial Intelligent Life and Christian Belief. *Philosophia Christi* 23, no. 1, 101–24.

McMullin, Ernan (2000). Life and Intelligence Far from Earth: Formulating Theological Issues. In Steven J. Dick, ed., *Many Worlds: The New Universe, Extraterrestrial Life and the Theological Implications*, Radnor, PA: Templeton Foundation Press, 151–76.

Moshenska, Gabriel (2017). Alternative Archaeologies. In Gabriel Moshenska, ed., *Key Concepts in Public Archaeology*, London: UCL Press, 122–37.

Nahin, Paul J. (2014). *Holy Sci-Fi!: Where Science Fiction and Religion Intersect*, New York: Springer.

Oderberg, David. S. (2014). Could there be a Superhuman Species? *The Southern Journal of Philosophy* 52, no. 2, 206–26.

O'Neill, Seamus (2018). Why the Imago Dei is in the Intellect Alone: A Criticism of a Phenomenology of Sensible Experience for Attaining an Image of God. *The Saint Anselm Journal* 13, no. 2, 19–41.

Paine, Thomas (1794). *The Age of Reason: Being an Investigation of True and Fabulous Theology*, Paris: Barrois.

Palmer, Susan J. (2004). *Aliens Adored: Raël's UFO Religion*, New Brunswick, NJ: Rutgers University Press.

Pandey, Nandini B. (2013). Caesar's Comet, the Julian Star, and the Invention of Augustus. *Transactions of the American Philological Association* 143, no. 2, 405–49. https://doi.org/10.1353/apa.2013.0010.

Pasulka, Diana. W. (2019). *American Cosmic: UFOs, Religion, Technology*, New York: Oxford University Press.

Peck, Steven L. (2015). *Wandering Realities: The Mormonish Short Fiction of Steven L. Peck*, Provo, Utah: Zarahemla Books.

Peters, Ted (2009). 'Astrotheology and the ETI Myth'. *Theology and Science* 7, no. 1, 3–30.

Peters, Ted (2014). *UFOs - God's Chariots?: Spirituality, Ancient Aliens, and Religious Yearnings in the Age of Extraterrestrials*, Pompton Plains: New Page Books.

Peterson, Gregory (1999). Religion and Science in *Star Trek: The Next Generation*: God, Q, and Evolutionary Eschatology on the Final Frontier. In Jennifer E. Porter and Darcee L. McLaren, eds., *Star Trek and Sacred Ground: Explorations of Star Trek, Religion, and American Culture*, Albany, NY: State University of New York Press, 61–76.

Peterson, Michael L. (2022). *Monotheism, Suffering, and Evil*, Cambridge: Cambridge University Press.

Playford, Richard (2024). The Alien in the Lamp? The Djinn and Alien Life in Islamic Theology. In Shoaib Ahmed Malik and Jörg Matthias Determann, eds., *Islamic Theology and Extraterrestrial Life: New Frontiers in Science and Religion*, London: I.B. Tauris, 159–73.

Polkinghorne, John. C. (1989). *Science and Providence* London: SPCK

The Qur'an: Sahih International Translation (1997). translated by Umm Muhammad, Mary Kennedy and Amatullah Bantley, Dar Abul Qasim: Saudi Arabia.

Reese, Gregory L. (2007). *UFO Religions: Inside Flying Saucer Cults and Culture*, London: I. B. Tauris.

Renfrew, Colin (2007). *Prehistory: The Making of the Human Mind*, New York: Modern Library.

Rig Veda (1896) Translated by Ralph T. H. Griffith. www.sacred-texts.com/hin/rigveda/index.htm [Accessed 26 April 2023].

Rothstein, Mikael (2009). 'His Name was Xenu. He Used Renegades ...': Aspects of Scientology's Founding Myth. In James R. Lewis, ed., *Scientology*, New York: Oxford University Press, 365–87.

Rothstein, Mikael (2021). The Aetherius Society: A Ritual Perspective. In Benjamin E. Zeller, ed., *Handbook of UFO Religions*, Leiden: Brill, 452–71

Roush, Wade (2020). *Extraterrestrials*, Cambridge, MA: MIT Press.

Russell, Mary Doria (1996). *The Sparrow*, New York: Villard Books.

Sagan, Carl (1985). *Contact*, New York: Simon & Schuster.

Sandberg, Anders, Eric Drexler, and Toby Ord (2018). Dissolving the Fermi Paradox. https://arxiv.org/abs/1806.02404.

Schmiechen, Peter (2005). *Saving Power: Theories of Atonement and Forms of the Church*, Michigan: Wm. B. Eerdmans.

Shatz, David. (2021). Science, Theology, and the Purpose of Creation. *Tradition: A Journal of Orthodox Jewish Thought* 53, no. 3, 250–9.

Sheth, Noel. (2004). 'Buddhism and Science' Presented to the *Science and Religion in Context Conference*, Hosted by the Metanexus Institute, Philadelphia, USA. www.metanexus.net/archive/conference2004/pdf/sheth.pdf [Accessed 25 April 2023].

Shivanandam M. (2015). 'Mercury Propulsion System in Vedic Vimanas and Modern Spacecrafts', *International Journal of Research and Analytical Reviews* 2, no. 2, 136–44.

Shostak, Seth (2009). *Confessions of an Alien Hunter: A Scientist's Search for Extraterrestrial Intelligence*, Washington, DC: National Geographic Society.

Signs (2002). directed by M. Night Shyamalan: Touchstone Pictures

Sitchin, Zechariah (1976). *The Twelfth Planet*, New York: Stein and Day.

Smith, Joseph ([1844] 1971). The King Follett Sermon. *Ensign* 1, no. 4. www
.churchofjesuschrist.org/study/ensign/1971/04/the-king-follett-sermon?
lang=eng.

Story, Ronald D. (1976). *The Space-Gods Revealed: A Close Look at the
Theories of Erich von Däniken*, New York: Barnes and Noble.

Sullivan, Francis A. (1992). *Salvation Outside the Church?: Tracing the
History of the Catholic Response*, London: Geoffrey Chapman.

Thuan, Trinh. Xuan. (2001). Cosmic Design from a Buddhist Perspective.
Annals of the New York Academy of Sciences 950, no. 1, 206–14.

Tsoukalos, Giorgio (2016). The Megaliths. In The Producers of Ancient Aliens,
ed., *Ancient Aliens: The Official Companion Book*, San Francisco, CA:
HarperOne, 83–96.

Tumminia, Diana G. (2005). *When Prophecy Never Fails: Myth and Reality in
a Flying-Saucer Group*, New York: Oxford University Press.

Tumminia, Diana G., and William H. Swatos (eds.) (2001). *How Prophecy
Lives*, Leiden: Brill.

The Uddhava Gita. (2000). Translated and edited by Manisha Wilmette Brown
and, Ambikananda Saraswati. Frances Lincoln: London.

Urban, Hugh (2011). *The Church of Scientology: A History of a New Religion*,
Princeton, NJ: Princeton University Press.

von Däniken, Erich (2017). *The Gods Never Left Us*, Newburyport, MA: New
Page.

von Däniken, Erich ([1968] 2019). *Chariots of the Gods? Was God an
Astronaut?* London: Souvenir Press.

von Däniken, Erich ([1999] 2019). Foreword from the 1999 Edition. In
Chariots of the Gods? Was God an Astronaut? London: Souvenir Press.

von Däniken, Erich (2019). Foreword (2018). In *Chariots of the Gods? Was
God an Astronaut?* London: Souvenir Press.

Ward, Blaze (2020). *The Assassin*, Seattle, WA: Knotted Road Press.

Ward, Peter and Brownlee, Donald E. (2000). *Rare Earth: Why Complex Life is
Uncommon in the Universe*, New York: Copernicus.

Weintraub, David A. (2014). *Religions and Extraterrestrial Life: How Will We
Deal With It?* Cham: Springer.

Wickramasinghe, Chandra. (2014). Life in the Universe: Concordance with
Buddhist Thought. *Journal of Oriental Studies* 24, pp. 201–12.

Wisdom, John (1945). Gods. *Proceedings of the Aristotelian Society* 45,
185–206

Yamamoto, Shuichi. and Kuwahara, Victor. S. (2008). Modern Cosmology and
Buddhism. *Journal of Oriental Studies* 18, 124–31.

Yoga Vasishtha of Valmiki (1891–1899) (4 volumes & unabridged) (1998). Translated by Vihārilāla Mitra and edited by Dr. Ravi Prakash Arya (1st ed.), Delhi: Parimal Publications.

Zeller, Benjamin E. (2014). *Heaven's Gate: America's UFO Religion*, New York: New York University Press.

Zeller, Benjamin E. (2021). *Handbook of UFO Religions*, Leiden: Brill.

Acknowledgements

This Element was written as part of the 'Religion and Astrobiology in Culture and Society' (RACS) research project, generously supported by a subgrant from the University of Birmingham's 'International Research Network for the Study of Science & Belief in Society' (INSBS), funded by the Templeton Religion Trust. At Birmingham, we especially wish to thanks Prof. Fern Elsdon-Baker, Dr Alex Hall, and Dr Stephen Jones for their support and encouragement.

RACS is a collaboration between St Mary's University (UK), the Lanier Theological Library (USA), Leeds Trinity University (UK), and the University of Notre Dame (Australia). Find us online at: https://racsnetwork.org and https://www.youtube.com/@racsnetwork8963

The authors would also collectively like to thank Heather Playford for her help with our website, branding, and YouTube channel, as well as her companionship throughout the course of this project. Consider yourself the fourth musketeer!

Cambridge Elements ≡

The Problems of God

Series Editor
Michael L. Peterson
Asbury Theological Seminary

Michael L. Peterson is Professor of Philosophy at Asbury Theological Seminary. He is the author of *God and Evil* (Routledge); *Monotheism, Suffering, and Evil* (Cambridge University Press); *With All Your Mind* (University of Notre Dame Press); *C. S. Lewis and the Christian Worldview* (Oxford University Press); *Evil and the Christian God* (Baker Book House); and *Philosophy of Education: Issues and Options* (Intervarsity Press). He is co-author of *Reason and Religious Belief* (Oxford University Press); *Science, Evolution, and Religion: A Debate about Atheism and Theism* (Oxford University Press); and *Biology, Religion, and Philosophy* (Cambridge University Press). He is editor of *The Problem of Evil: Selected Readings* (University of Notre Dame Press). He is co-editor of *Philosophy of Religion: Selected Readings* (Oxford University Press) and *Contemporary Debates in Philosophy of Religion* (Wiley-Blackwell). He served as General Editor of the Blackwell monograph series Exploring Philosophy of Religion and is founding Managing Editor of the journal *Faith and Philosophy*.

About the Series

This series explores problems related to God, such as the human quest for God or gods, contemplation of God, and critique and rejection of God. Concise, authoritative volumes in this series will reflect the methods of a variety of disciplines, including philosophy of religion, theology, religious studies, and sociology.

Cambridge Elements ☰

The Problems of God

A full series listing is available at: www.cambridge.org/EPOG.

Printed in the United States
by Baker & Taylor Publisher Services